*Ingredients for Peace*
is dedicated to all who work for peace
in the belief that some day,
all people will live in a world
of peace, justice and equality,
where they will be able to
share their favorite meals
with family and friends everyday -
and not just dream about it.

# INTRODUCTION
*Emily Goose & Jody Williams*

*From Emily:*

An idea sparked by an exciting conversation at the dinner table has, over the past year and a half, evolved from a school project – a mandatory undertaking with deadlines, presentations, and bi-weekly journal entries – to something that I will forever hold as not only an accomplishment, but as the beginning of a new chapter in my life.

Every senior at my high school, Fredericksburg Academy in Fredericksburg, Virginia, is required to create a "senior exhibit." Each student chooses a topic and embarks on a journey to complete a project around the topic while thoroughly reflecting on personal growth, struggles, and new knowledge obtained in the process.

At dinner one evening, we (me, Jody, and my Dad, Steve Goose, who is also a recipe contributor) began brainstorming project ideas. As editor of my school yearbook, I had quite a bit of experience with layout and design and wanted to do a project that would further hone those skills. With the snap of a finger we had it figured out – a cookbook with recipes from peacemakers around the world. We began jotting down possible contributors, possible titles, sketching cover ideas and more. And from then on, we've been determined.

Jody's job was getting recipe contributions and quotes from her peace activist friends and colleagues. Mine was creating the book from cover to cover – organizing, formatting, and creating pages for every contributor. Then I had it made on Lulu.com, a self-publishing website, for my presentation in front of a quarter of my high school. Sure I explained the hard work of making the cookbook, but I was probably more excited to talk about what I had gotten out of it – which was inspiration. While the cookbook today hardly resembles the cookbook I had on my presentation day (after multiple changes, editing sessions with Jody, tweaking of elements and re-creation of pages), in essence, the book's meaning remains the same for me.

*Ingredients for Peace* is more than my senior exhibit. It has been a joyful, fun and rewarding experience for me. Not only do I feel like I've "gotten to know" amazing contributors from all over the world, but I've gained knowledge on worldly topics, global issues, and most importantly – I've become aware of and a part of a quest toward something so precious as peace. I am honored to be a part of this cookbook and honored to now have such an insight into the purpose that unites these people. Working to develop this cookbook opened my eyes to so many things – perhaps the most important being that whatever I pursue in the future, I want a huge part of my life to be focused on giving back and helping those in need, being an active and aware citizen, and working hard to make the difference that we all see and know there is a need for: promoting peace.

*From Jody:*

When Emily settled on this cookbook idea for her senior project, I have to admit I was totally thrilled. For many reasons. But not the least of which is that for years I tried to get together a recipe group – activist friends to share recipes of food that they love. Frankly, it was a bust. This cookbook, for me, was a different vehicle for wresting recipes from very busy people. But even getting a single recipe wasn't as easy at it seems like it would be. And quotes about food and peace on top of that....well, I wasn't always successful. Mostly because I forgot to ask and then nag!

Kvetching aside, working with Emily to create this end product has been a wonderful experience. We both deeply appreciate the generosity of each and every person who took the time to contribute. It was fun seeing what people would choose to send in and very interesting and moving to read some of the quotes that they also wrote.

When Emily did the cookbook first for her school project, the sections she did about each contributor were mostly bits of information that she could find on the web – although she does know some of the people quite well, and not just me and her father! But when we started reworking the cookbook for a (hopefully) broader audience, we thought it could be interesting if I wrote the short "peace bios" and made them more personal, more human – since everyone who has contributed is someone I know and have worked with.

In first coming up with the list of possible contributors, we wanted people who are involved in various kinds of work, all of which are elements of building sustainable peace. There are human rights activists and disarmament types – from landmines and cluster bombs to nuclear bombs. There are people who work with refugee populations and those who try innovative means of conflict resolution. There are activists who do not believe nuclear energy is either "clean" or "sustainable." There are those who work for environmental justice and others supporting international humanitarian law.

In their "peace bios" we hope to demonstrate in brief these various ways of contributing to building a world of sustainable peace with justice and equality. We've provided web information for organizations that each work with to give readers access to lots and lots of information about any number of issues. If you go to these websites and click onto the links that most provide you can learn as much as you could possibly want about the broad networks of people working together for a better world. Also, you can "google" the names of the contributors and find even more information on them and their work.

Emily and I hope you enjoy going through the cookbook as much as we've enjoyed bringing the pages to you. We apologize in advance for any errors or omissions you find. Neither of us are professionals in the book world, to say the least! But we've tried to make the cookbook as error free as possible. In fact, each of us has gone over each page so many times that by now we should have the entire book memorized!

Finally, in buying this cookbook, you are contributing to the work of the Nobel Women's Initiative or the work to eradicate landmines and cluster bombs. So, not only do you get some awesome recipes and good leads for information about many of the issues facing us in our world today, but also you are helping make the world a better place with your contribution.

Thanks! And most of all – E N J O Y!

# Table of Contents

| | | |
|---|---|---|
| Jose de Arteaga | Papito and Abuelo's Chicken Fricasee | 1 |
| Simona Beltrami | Impanata de Carciofi (Artichoke Pie) | 3 |
| Liz Bernstein | Dad's Gazpacho | 6 |
| | Estelle's Pecan Pie | 6 |
| Alison Bock | Breaded Pork Tenderloin | 8 |
| Lydia Cladek | Green Pudding | 10 |
| | Tomatoes Stuffed with Not-Cheese | 10 |
| Robi Damelin | Sinful Chocolate | 12 |
| Bob Eaton | Smoked Salmon Pizza or Proscuiutto Pizza with Killer Pizza Dough | 14 |
| Shirin Ebadi | Shirin's Healthy Four Bean Mélange | 17 |
| Mette Eliseussen | Spinach Soup | 19 |
| Dawn Engle & Ivan Suvanjieff | Chicken with Grapes and White Cream Sauce | 21 |
| Eve Ensler | Activist Pasta | 24 |
| Shirin Ershadi | Persian Cucumber-Mint Yogurt | 25 |
| Mia Farrow | Mia's Awesome Pancakes | 26 |
| Allison Fisher | Monday Night Post-Yoga Smoothie | 28 |
| Jessica Gabrian | Peace Bean Salad | 29 |
| Emily Goose | Chocolate Mousse (-or Cake) | 32 |
| | Hollandaise Sauce | 33 |
| Stephen Goose | Sesame Beef | 34 |
| | Goose's Fabulous BBQ Sauce | 35 |
| | Grilled Flank Steak Teriyaki | 35 |
| | Potatoes Gruyère | 36 |
| | Sautéed Green Beans with Garlic | 37 |
| Paul Hannon | Granny McGain's Fruit Sauce | 39 |
| & Maureen Hollingworth | Granddaughters' Zucchini Relish | 40 |
| Peter Herby | Saffron Chicken | 42 |
| Felicity Hill | Lemon Risotto | 44 |
| Mark Hiznay | Cheese Fondue | 47 |
| Brigid Inder | Sudanese Eggplant Salad | 50 |
| Aimee Jachym | Go-Chu Mac and Cheese | 52 |
| | Kimchi Quesadillas | 53 |
| Anotnia Juhasz | Roasted Corn Broth with Chunky Pea Guacamole | 54 |

| | | |
|---|---|---|
| **Cele Keeper** | Erna Sass's Seafood Gumbo | 56 |
| **Colleen Kelly** | Mrs. Thrasher's Apple Pie | 58 |
| **Rebecca Larson** | Winter Wassail | 60 |
| **Barbara Lawton** | Fresh Fig Tart with Rosemary Cornmeal Crust and Lemon Mascarpone Cream | 62 |
| **Nang Lao Liang Won** | Coconut Rice | 64 |
| | Chicken Curry | 64 |
| | Burmese-Style Shallot Salad | 65 |
| **Wangari Maathai** | Stewed Spinach & Amaranth | 66 |
| | Mataha (Red Beans, Corn and Potatoes) | 66 |
| **Mairead Maguire** | Pavlova | 68 |
| **Jim McGovern** | Aunt Jerry McGovern's Guiness Stew | 70 |
| **Mary Ellen McNish** | Brunch Casserole | 72 |
| **Rigoberta Menchù Tum** | Chilim (Pork Ribs with Tomatoes and Chile) | 74 |
| **Pat Mitchell** | Grandmother's Red Velvet Cake | 76 |
| **Princess Dina & Prince Mired Ra'ad** | Mujadara (Rice, Lentils & Onions) | 78 |
| **José Ramos-Horta** | Timorese Fish Balls | 80 |
| **Judy Rand** | Chicken Dijon with Capers | 82 |
| | Mango-Avocado Salsa | 82 |
| **Markus Reiterer** | Mediterranean Bread Roll | 84 |
| **John Rodsted** | The Brew is the Bog & the Bog is a Brew, from John to You | 86 |
| **Julianna Roosevelt** | Blueberry (Huckleberry) Pudding | 89 |
| **Sima Samar** | Qabuli Palau (Chicken with Basmati Rice & Carrots) | 91 |
| **Nora Sheets & her Fourth Grade "Proud Students Against Landmines"** | Beets, Love and Understanding | 94 |
| | Whirled Peas (Split Pea Soup) | 94 |
| | "Paz" the Cookies | 95 |
| | Let There be Pesto (Pesto Spaghetti Squash) | 95 |
| | Give Peas a Chance (Old Fashioned Creamed Peas) | 96 |

| | | |
|---|---|---|
| **Emily Simon** | Salmon Curry | 97 |
| | The Best Rice You Will Ever Eat | 98 |
| **Satnam Singh** | Chicken Marsala Delhi Style | 99 |
| | Garam Masala | 100 |
| **Susannah Sirkin** | Mesas Con Frescas en la Nieve | 102 |
| | (Tables with Strawberries in Snow) | |
| | Ambrosia (The food of the gods | 102 |
| | that humans deserve) | |
| **Cornelio Sommaruga** | Risotto Alla Luganese | 103 |
| **Desmond Tutu** | Tutu Chicken | 105 |
| **Lynne Twist** | Carrot-Tomato-Lentil-Soup | 107 |
| **Mario Velasquez** | Central American Guacamole | 109 |
| **Lisa Veneklasen** | The Ultimate Comfort Squash | 111 |
| **Mary Wareham** | Friands (Sweet Cakes) | 113 |
| | Pavlova for Peace | 114 |
| **Cora Weiss** | Peace Soup | 116 |
| **Gloria White-Hammond** | Banana Cake Cockaigne | 118 |
| **Betty Williams** | Salmon in Pastry | 120 |
| **Jody Williams** | South Asian Meatloaf | 122 |
| | Fantastic Bourbon Apple Pie | 124 |
| **Zeina Zataari** | The Perfect Baba Ghanouj | 126 |
| **Qing Zhang** | Shrimp Balls in Tofu | 128 |

# JOSE DE ARTEAGA

Casa de Arteaga
Taverna y restaurante de primera categoria
Favorite Recipes

## Papito and Abuelo's Chicken Fricasee

*Ingredients:*

*For Sofrito (sauce):*

¼ cup olive oil

2-inch long piece of Spanish chorizo (spicy sausage), sliced; (if you can't find Spanish chorizo, use about ¼ pound smoked ham, diced)

1 stalk celery, chopped

1 large green pepper, chopped

1 large onion, chopped

4-6 cloves garlic, chopped

2 envelopes Goya sazon (either flavor seasoning packet achiote/cilantro or azafran)

1 or 2 8-ounce cans tomato sauce (try one first and see if it needs more)

Water – start with 1½ cups and add more if needed to make enough sauce for the chicken

*For the rest:*

Chicken cut into serving pieces and skinned – two pieces per person and extras if you want leftovers

2-3 small bay leaves

Potatoes, quartered – 1 per person

Carrots, cut into about 2-inch pieces -- about ½ carrot per person

Capers and stuffed green olives – as many as you like; wash them first because they are so salty

Chopped cilantro, minced – a few sprigs

Oregano, adobo, salt and pepper, to taste

¼ cup Sherry wine

## Preparation:

1. For the Sofrito: Heat olive oil and sauté chorizo, celery, pepper, onion and garlic until soft. Add Goya seasoning packets, tomato sauce and water. Taste for seasoning and adjust. It should be a little saltier than you like because the chicken will take up the salt.

2. Add the chicken, bay leaves, potatoes, carrots, capers, olives, cilantro, oregano, adobo, salt and pepper, and wine. Simmer until tender. (Once you've added the chicken, you should not taste the sauce again until it is well cooked.) You can add more sauce and water after the chicken and other ingredients, depending on how saucy you want the finished dish.

*Serve over white rice & enjoy.*

## About the Contributor...

Jose de Arteaga is an advocate, activist and attorney with a wild sense of humor and a burning desire for social change. Since 2004, he has dedicated his passion, commitment and years of experience to Landmines Blow!, a grassroots non-governmental organization that builds public awareness about the impact of landmines and cluster bombs and raises money to help build wells for safe drinking water in mine-affected communities. Jose is its vice-president. For more information about Landmines Blow!, which among other things is a member of the International Campaign to Ban Landmines, and Jose de Arteaga, including photos, check out: www.landminesblow.com. (In his spare time, Jose is a program manager for the District of Columbia's Department of Human Services. He's also an excellent dancer.)

# SIMONA BELTRAMI

*"I think the recipe will need some native cook's edit, as I am more comfortable in English with terminology for sensor fuzes than for baking (there is something fundamentally wrong with the world, obviously). The transfer of ancient Sardinian cooking wisdom into modern English-speaking cookery has proven a bit of a challenge!"*

## Impanata de Carciofi
## (Artichoke Pie)
### (Serves four)

*Ingredients:*

Filling:
- 14 ounces diced beef
- 8 artichokes
- 2 small tomatoes
- Saffron
- 2 tablespoons olive oil
- 1 clove garlic
- Stock
- Salt to taste

Pastry:
- 2 cups flour
- 4 tablespoons butter
- Water
- Pinch of salt

*Preparation:*

1. **The night before preparing the dish,** put the meat in a bowl, covered in stock, adding the clove of garlic, the saffon and the two tomatoes finely chopped. Leave to infuse overnight.

2. Preheat oven to 350°F.

3. Remove the outer leaves and thorns from the artichokes and cut the hearts in fine slices. You can add the stems (chopped) after removing the thick outer skin. As you slice them, put the artichokes in a bowl with water and a dash of vinegar, which prevents them from turning black.

4. Add the artichokes to the meat and stock and then add the olive oil, mixing well. Add salt to taste. Set aside.

*The pastry shell:*

5. Melt the butter in a small saucepan and let cool.

6. Make a flour mound on a wooden board, scoop a "well" in the middle, add a pinch of salt and pour the cooled, melted butter and enough water to make a dough into the "well." Knead the dough and leave it to "rest" for 20 minutes, covering it with a tea towel.

7. Flatten the dough to form a thin crust. Divide the crust in two parts – one for the bottom and the other for the top of the pie.

8. Put the bottom of the crust in a pie pan and fill it with the meat, stock and artichoke filling, ensuring that it remains moist. (The stock must be level with the meat and artichoke filling.) Close the pie with the top crust and seal the edges well.

9. Cook for 2½ hours. If the pastry turns brown too quickly, cover it with foil to protect it from the heat.

*Serve and enjoy!*

## About the Contributor...

Simona Beltrami currently serves as the Advocacy Director of the International Campaign to Ban Landmines - the ICBL - and before that was the dynamic, creative Coordinator of the Italian Campaign to Ban Landmines. Simona brought her formidable skills to the landmine movement from other advocacy work, including years with Amnesty International. For landmine work, Italy was an important country to convince to ban the weapon because at the time of the 1992 launch of the ICBL, it was one of the biggest producers and exporters of landmines in the world. The ICBL is a global coalition of non-governmental organizations that spearheaded the effort that achieved its goal of a treaty banning landmines in 1997; for that work it received the Nobel Peace Prize that same year. With her wit and warmth in at least three languages, Simona inspires campaigners to work hard to ensure that the ICBL remains vibrant in its commitment to make sure that the Mine Ban Treaty is obeyed, landmines are removed from the ground, and appropriate care is provided to all landmine survivors. You'll find a ton of information about the ICBL at: www.icbl.org.

# LIZ
# BERNSTEIN

"I grew up in New Orleans and learned to cook watching my dad, chopping vegetables as his 'sous chef.' Gazpacho needed a lot of chopped vegetables – in it and for the garnish. I've always loved gazpacho – the very idea of the cold soup on a hot day is refreshing, whether in New Orleans, hot and humid much of the year, or now in Ottawa on a hot summer day – using the fresh seasonal vegetables from our local CSA farm (community supported agriculture) nearby that we buy a 'share' in at the start of the growing season and are rewarded with fresh veggies each week throughout the summer.

Though we may have different politics, I learned much about being a peace activist from my family. And about cooking – watching my dad. He rarely used a cookbook, and I chopped vegetables and watched. But he never baked, never made desserts or anything sweet. I started baking, making cookies and cakes, when I was a kid. Since I couldn't learn from watching him, I turned to cookbooks – my Betty Crocker toy kitchen and oven was one of my favorites. I graduated from the toy cakes to real ones pretty fast. I just followed along exactly what they said, ½ cup of this, 1 cup of that, carefully measuring, pouring, stirring… I never understood when adults said, 'You're such a good baker!' It was like yeah, I can follow instructions pretty well, can't you? What's the big deal? If you just follow what's written down in the book, doesn't it always turn out right?

They say the French created pecan pie soon after settling in New Orleans – once the Native Americans introduced them to pecans. I made Estelle's Pecan Pie from an old out-of-print New Orleans cookbook we tried unsuccessfully to trace. We don't know who Estelle is so let's just say it's 'traditional.' I followed it to the letter, even using the name brand 'Karo corn syrup' – before the days of our concern of corn taking over our food and us being made up of 65% corn…. We all still make it every Thanksgiving.

I didn't realize 'til much later I'd learned much more form my dad than the cookbooks. I still cook using both – intuition and improvisation as well as the basic guide. And I think you need both for good peace work: some basic ingredients of an analysis, strategy, action plan with some solid organizing and communication tools. But you also have to be flexible, creative, making the most of what's at hand – in the fridge or the political land-scape – and not get hung up on what's missing. Have confidence; try it, if it doesn't work, adapt, try something else. Persist. There are some basics, but no cookie-cutter approach!"

# Dad's Gazpacho

*Ingredients:*

**4-5 ripe tomatoes (or if you're stuck, a 16-ounce can of seasoned diced tomatoes will do)**
**1 green pepper**
**1 red pepper (if averse to domineering green peppers, another red/yellow will do instead)**
**Several scallions**
**1 small Vidalia or red onion**
**1-2 carrots**
**1-2 celery stalks**
**1 cucumber**
**Several garlic cloves**
**1 tablespoon olive oil**
**2 tablespoons of your preferred vinegar**
**1 splash of fresh lemon juice**
**Add to taste: oregano, basil, parsley, salt and pepper**

*Preparation:*

1. Slightly chop all the vegetables, then put them in food processor and purée at high speed in many short spurts. If it's not your preferred consistency or temperature, either add room temperature stock or stir in ice cubes or let it sit in the fridge/freezer to get cold enough.

2. Chop up some accompaniments: chopped fresh tomato, chopped/diced celery, peppers, cucumber, parsley, and add as you like!

*Bon appétit!*

# Estelle's Pecan Pie

*Ingredients:*

**3 eggs**
**¾ cup sugar**
**1 teaspoon vanilla**
**1 cup white (Karo) corn syrup**
**½ stick butter or margarine**
**1 cup pecans, coarsely chopped**
**9-inch pie shell (homemade or store bought – unbaked)**

## Preparation:

1. Preheat oven to 350°F.

2. Combine eggs, sugar, corn syrup. Add melted butter and vanilla. Then add pecans.

3. Pour into unbaked pie shell.

4. Bake for 45-50 minutes. Check pie at 25 minutes and turn if necessary for even baking.

5. Let cool, then refrigerate overnight.

## About the Contributor...

Liz Bernstein came to her current position as the Executive Director of the Nobel Women's Initiative (NWI) through a circuitous route that took her from working in Cambodian refugee camps on the border with Thailand to taking over as coordinator of the ICBL in February 1998, operating first from Mozambique, then Washington and finally Ottawa until the end of 2004. Before helping launch the NWI in January 2006 as its founding director, she coordinated the Make Poverty History campaign in Canada. The Nobel Women's Initiative is an effort by sister Nobel Peace Laureates Jody Williams, Shirin Ebadi, Wangari Maathai, Rigoberta Menchú Tum, Betty Williams, and Mairead Maguire to promote the work of women's rights activists to advance peace with justice and equality for women and all peoples in this world. For more information about NWI, please go to: www.nobelwomensinitiative.org.

Brilliant is not a word to be used cavalierly. Liz is a brilliant strategist and organizer who has been and is mentor to "legions" of emerging activists. In her spare time she created an NGO in Ottawa, where she lives. "Ecology Ottawa" works "to promote citizen participation in decisions that shape Ottawa's environment and to hold the city council accountable for its environmental performance."
Check it out at: www.ecologyottawa.ca.

# ALISON BOCK

*"This recipe is for breaded pork tenderloin – one of my personal favs from back in the day. My grandma used to make tons of it when we went on vacation; we would take it to have on a roadside picnic. It never made it outside the state of Illinois, though, because we would all eat our sandwiches within the first hour of the car ride! No wonder I looked like a potato dumpling growing up – although my grandma lived well into her 80s and never worried about cholesterol! I guess this would be something we could take along for the ride while scoping out new locations to build wells in landmine-affected communities..."*

## Breaded Pork Tenderloin

### Ingredients:

**2 pounds of pork shoulder**
**Flour**
**3 eggs**
**Bread crumbs**
**Salt**
**Oil or margarine**
*For gravy:*
**2 cans of cream of mushroom soup**
**Milk**

### Preparation:

1. Preheat oven to 350°F.

2. Slice each pork shoulder about one eighth of an inch thick, then flatten or pound with a wooden mallet (or any mallet).

3. Prepare three pie plates with the following: one with flour, one with 2 well-beaten eggs and one with fine bread crumbs.

4. Salt the meat. Dip each slice in flour, then eggs, then the bread crumbs.

5. Fry slowly in ½ inch of oil or margarine until golden brown on both sides.

6. Place in a casserole dish and bake for 30 minutes.

7. For gravy, add 2 cans of cream of mushroom soup and one can of milk to frying pan, scraping browned pieces in bottom of pan.

*Pork chops, pork tenderloin, chicken pieces or beef liver can also be prepared this way. This is wonderful served with dumplings and sauerkraut.*

## About the Contributor...

Alison Bock is the president and founder of Landmines Blow!, which she created in 2003 to raise awareness of landmines and their impact on civilians. Wild and woolly and with a mind that works overtime, Alison – conspiring with Landmines Blow!'s vice-president Jose de Arteaga and with the support of people like teacher Nora Sheets and her fourth grade "Proud Students Against Landmines" – broadened the organization's mission to include raising money to build wells in mined communities in Cambodia. Almost half of all villages there contain landmines and 9.5 million Cambodian inhabitants do not have access to clean drinking water. Alison has years of advocacy/activist experience including serving as a team captain for AIDS Walk Chicago from 1990-95, raising over $200,000 to benefit AIDS research. For fifteen years before founding Landmines Blow!, she worked as a communications professional in the healthcare industry in Chicago, Illinois. Like her pal and colleague Jose de Atreaga, Alison Bock can dance. Check out Landmines Blow! at: www.landminesblow.com.

# LYDIA CLADEK

*"Raw food is a gorgeous way to nourish yourself. It is completely peaceful, amazingly healthful, nutrient dense, and, enjoyed regularly, makes you even more beautiful. So says Tonya Zavasta, who has written several books on raw food.*

*There is one thing about raw food – soaking is often involved, which means planning a day or more ahead. So is dehydrating, which takes equipment and time. It involves strange ingredients – raw soy sauce, for example – and lots of chopping. So what! In her book, Uncooked Creations, Tonya Zavasta says you see a change in your appearance in just three months.*

*That said, here are two favorite recipes that are easy and quick to prepare.*

*Green pudding is inspired by Tonya. She served it at a workshop on raw foods and I was hooked. (She's fifty, looked forty, skin glowing and a teeny waist.) It looks weird, tastes surprisingly delicious and is so healthful. I enjoy it warm, right from the blender."*

## Green Pudding

*Ingredients:*

**One medium to large chilled mango**
**1 cup loosely packed kale**

*Preparation:*

1. Chop kale.
2. Peel and cut mango into bite-size pieces.
3. Blend in blender or food processor until fully blended.
4. Serve immediately or chill.

## Tomatoes Stuffed with Not-Cheese

*Ingredients:*

**½ cup raw unsalted cashews**
**½ cup raw unsalted pine nuts**
**2 tablespoons lemon juice**
**1 cup loosely packed basil, chopped**
**½ teaspoon salt**
**½ teaspoon pepper**
**¼ to ½ cup water**
**1 dozen Campari tomatoes or large cherry tomatoes**

## Preparation:

1. Cut tops of tomatoes off. Hull out and drain upside down on a paper towel. Set aside.

2. In bowl of food processor – grind cashews and pine nuts until a fine powder. Gradually add water, starting with ¼ cup. Add lemon juice, basil, salt and pepper. You may need to add more water to get desired consistency, nearly as thick as ricotta cheese.

3. Stuff tomatoes and garnish with fresh basil leaf.

4. Refrigerate until serving or serve immediately.

*You can use whatever fresh herbs you may have on hand, or other raw nuts as well. For example: fresh oregano, fresh dill or raw macadamia nuts. You can also use different vegetables to stuff – like English cucumber cups.*

## About the Contributor...

Lydia Cladek is a generous and experienced philanthropist with a strong and deep commitment to supporting efforts to better our world. Among other work, Lydia is a supporter of the Nobel Women's Initiative and was a member of the NWI "Women for Peace" delegation in July-August 2008 which met with Burmese women refugees along the Burma-Thailand border and then Sudanese women in both South Sudan and Darfur refugee camps in Chad. Her calm spirit and wry and unique sense of humor were fantastic aspects Lydia brought to the mix of a fabulous group of women on the delegation. The Nobel Women's Initiative was founded by sister Nobel Peace Laureates Jody Williams, Shirin Ebadi, Wangari Maathai, Rigoberta Menchú Tum, Betty Williams, and Mairead Maguire in January 2006. Please see: www.nobelwomensinitiative.org. When she's not helping save the world, Lydia Cladek is a very successful businesswoman who lives in Florida.

# ROBI DAMELIN

*"I am dashing off to South Africa today, so excited is not the word, have not been there for some 28 years… swore I would never go back, never say never. This recipe is guaranteed to ruin any home of normal cholesterol, and let's call it 'Sinful Chocolate.'"*

## Sinful Chocolate

*Ingredients:*

**7 ounces unsweetened chocolate**
**1 cup sugar**
**1 stick butter**
**5 medium eggs**
**5 tablespoons self-rising flour**
**½ cup walnuts, chopped**

*Preparation:*

1. Preheat oven to 350°F.
2. Grease 9x13-inch baking tin.
3. Melt the butter, chocolate and sugar over low flame and stir constantly, then remove from heat.
4. Continue stirring, adding the eggs one at a time.
5. Stir in walnuts.
6. Fold in the flour.
7. Place in baking tin and bake for 20 minutes. When ready, it is still slightly moist.

*A little whipped cream on top would not be amiss.*

## About the Contributor...

Robi Damelin is originally from South Africa but lives in Israel. She is part of the Parents Circle-Families Forum, an organization made up of bereaved Israeli and Palestinian families, "victims from both sides, embark[ed] on a joint reconciliation mission while the conflict is still active." In March 2002, her twenty-eight-year-old son, David, was shot by a sniper at a checkpoint in the Occupied Territories while serving in the Israeli army. Like others, both Palestinian and Israeli, who did not want their pain and grief to be used to fuel the conflict, Damelin sought other routes and went to a Parents Circle-Families Forum symposium. As she says, the organization "soon became my lifeline." Robi is straightforward and determined and her commitment and work for peace and reconciliation is an example for us all. Please meet Robi Damelin and others from the Parents Circle-Families Forum at: www.theparentscircle.com.

# BOB EATON

*"I first got my start doing pizza as head baker at Allenwood Federal Prison – doing 25 months for refusing the draft during the Vietnam War. We made rectangular pizzas so they could be divided evenly and thus avoid food riots. It wasn't so much that our pizzas were that great – inmates just didn't need much to start a ruckus. It helped to break up the monotony.*

*Ninety percent of a great pizza is in the dough. This is a thin crust dough. Crispy on the outside and smooth and creamy on the inside. This recipe doesn't take much time, just forward planning. You start the dough the day before cooking."*

## Smoked Salmon Pizza or Prosciutto Pizza
### with
## "Killer" Pizza Dough
(With thanks to *The Bread Maker's Apprentice* by Peter Reinhart)

*Ingredients:*

5½ cups high gluten flour, i.e. bread flour
1¾ teaspoons salt
1 teaspoon instant yeast (better than active dry yeast; active dry will do)
¼ cup olive or vegetable oil
1¾ cups ice cold water
Semolina or corn meal for dusting

*Preparation:*

Phase One – 12-20 minutes

1. Mix all the ingredients together until smooth and really sticky – should barely pull away from the mixing bowl. I mix the dough using my hand. Turn it and squeeze it between your figures – like playing with mud when you were a kid. If it isn't really sticky to the touch, rinse hand in cold water and work the dough some more. If it gets so sticky you can't get your hand free of it, add a little flour.

2. Sprinkle flour on the table, roll the dough into a log and cut into six equal pieces. Roll each piece into a round ball and put on a well-greased piece of parchment paper on a cookie pan. Cover each ball with misted oil or hand applied oil, cover tray with plastic wrap and put into the refrigerator. It will keep nicely for up to three days.

Phase Two – Pizza day: Resting the dough – two hours

3. Take the dough out of the refrigerator two hours before cooking time and let it sit at room temperature – still covered up.

Phase Three – Pizza day: Shaping and cooking – 15 minutes

4. Preheat the oven as hot as it will go – it make take up to 45 minutes to get everything really hot. My oven only goes to 550°F, but 700°F is better. A pizza stone is a very good thing to have – if you own one, place in oven when you set the temperature so that it gets hot as the oven does.

5. Shape a ball into a flat disk about 8 inches in diameter. It should be pretty thing, a little less than a quarter of an inch thick. Try working the disc on top of your two balled hands and spinning it. If the dough keeps springing back, let it rest on the table while you take ten minutes for conversation with a friend and a glass of wine. After ten minutes, come back and try again.

6. Construct the pizza on top of a flat bread peel or a cookie baking sheet without a lip. Before putting the dough on the peel or pan, sprinkle with corn meal. This will help the dough slide off the peel or pan and into the oven. Use corn meal, not corn flour. Meal is slightly gritty and helps the slide and tastes great on the finished product.

7. Add toppings to your own taste:

Option 1: Smoked Salmon: Wendy's [Bob's wife, Wendy Batson] favorite is fresh dill, goat cheese and kalamatra olives. Once out of the oven, add smoked salmon and more fresh dill. A nice dry, white wine and you are into some serious business.

Option 2: Prosciutto: My favorite is any marbled or blue cheese – gorgonzola is very nice, and slices of prosciutto ham, which can be added before or after the cooking. Once out of the oven, top with fresh arugula lettuce. This combination was first discovered at Slice Pizza in south Philadelphia – I reckon Philly's greatest pizza joint. Worth a visit. Bring your own wine. (www.slicepa.com)

8. Once you have put the pizza together, slide off the peel or baking sheet onto the pizza stone in your now very hot oven. Cook about 5-7 minutes, until the edges bubble and get dark brown – even a little char is not bad.

## About the Contributor...

Bob Eaton is the Executive Director of the Survey Action Center, a non-governmental humanitarian organization that works toward the ultimate goal of a world free of the danger of landmines. A Quaker, Bob's decades of experience as a peace activist have only sharpened his unique observations on human nature and social change and honed his wry and pointed sense of humor. Bob's awareness of the landmine problem long pre-dates the birth of the International Campaign to Ban Landmines from his days working in Laos. His Survey Action Center works to provide accurate information about mined areas so mine clearance programs can prioritize clearance work. Bob Eaton, among many other things, believes in "accentuating the positive and eliminating the negative." The Survey Action Center and Bob Eaton can be found at: www.sac-na.org.

# SHIRIN EBADI

## Shirin's Healthy Four Bean Mélange

*Ingredients:*

- ¼ **cup red beans (red with black stripe)**
- ¼ **cup lentils**
- ¼ **cup garbanzo beans (chickpeas)**
- ¼ **cup small grey beans**
- ¼ **cup white beans (cannellini)**
- 2 **tablespoons balsamic vinegar**
- **Salt and pepper to taste**

*Preparation:*

1. Pick over dried beans and lentils and wash thoroughly. Barely cover with water and cook until water is absorbed and beans are soft.
2. Remove from heat and add salt, pepper and balsamic vinegar.

*This is refreshing served with orange or grapefruit juice.*

## About the Contributor...

Dr. Shirin Ebadi, one of the first women judges in Iran, is a lawyer, human rights activist, and prolific writer who, in 2003, became the first Muslim woman to receive the Nobel Peace Prize. She has founded various Iranian non-governmental organizations including the Defenders of Human Rights Center (DHRC)and the Organization for the Defense of Mine Victims, both closed down by the government in December of 2008, as part of her ongoing efforts to promote and protect human rights – particularly those of women and children – and to defend political prisoners. She has also been a fervent promoter of the "One Million Signatures Campaign," an effort spearheaded by Iranian women to reform law and achieve equal legal status in Iran. Despite continuing threats against her life, attacks on her organizations and her home and office, she is fearless in her unremitting fight for democracy, justice and equality in her country and in the world.

Shirin Ebadi first brought up the idea of the Nobel Women's Initiative when talking with Jody Williams at an international conference on landmines in Nairobi, Kenya at the end of 2004. The next day they discussed it when they met with Professor Wangari Maathai, who had become the twelfth woman to be awarded the Nobel Peace Prize only a few weeks earlier. With that discussion over tea, the commitment to a Nobel Women's Initiative was forged. The three were joined by Betty Williams, Rigoberta Menchú Tum and Mairead Maguire and NWI was launched in January 2006. Their sister Peace Laureate Aung San Suu Kyi has not been able to join NWI due to her continued imprisonment in Burma. For information about the One Million Signatures Campaign, go to: www.sign4change.info/english/. You can also find out more about Dr. Shirin Ebadi and some of her work at: www.nobelwomensinitiative.org.

# METTE
# ELISEUSSEN

*"To my surprise, food and cooking became important to me when I lived in Kabul in Afghanistan. Anywhere I went, I saw shattered lives and destroyed civilization. Sixty staff and I ran ourselves ragged among the rubble trying to beat the death statistics. There were twenty (and often more) incidents a week with landmines, cluster bombs and other remnants of war. We tried to teach the children how to survive. When the deminers were too busy and too tired to clear the land, we strived to create small but safe playgrounds. We tried so hard. To cope with too many lost limbs and lost lives, the rockets and the bombs, the never ending decrees of vice and virtue issued by the ruling Taliban, or the long lonesome evenings and nights during curfews and a lack of modern life, I turned to cooking.*

*I searched and found beauty in the vegetables, fruits and local foods that were available. There was always a lack of food as the city was under siege. Sometimes only a few lorries and donkeys were able to pass through the frontlines and arrive with their goods to the market. However, I soon realized that what I ate in Kabul was tastier and healthier than the food I used to eat back home. I felt the texture, I watched the color, and I discovered the shape and pattern of each and every ingredient as I prepared for the next meal. Cooking became soothing and it kept me going after I left the war and lived a post-conflict life.*

*I also discovered it was possible to ban landmines and cluster bombs, making peace possible without the most hazardous legacy from the war. I discovered paths and patterns used to ban the weapons were varied, creating a process where politicians, decision makers and civil society from countries across the world met, talked and changed history together. It feels good to be part of both processes.*

*Somehow we seemed to have an abundance of spinach in Kabul and I lived on Chicken Street where eggs were always around. Therefore, spinach soup with hard-boiled eggs was often on the menu."*

# Spinach Soup

*Ingredients:*

**2 onions**
**Garlic**
**1 potato**
**1 tomato**
**Chicken stock**
**Bunches of spinach**
**Cream (optional)**
**Salt and pepper to taste**
**Eggs**

*Preparation:*

1. Chop a couple of onions; sauté them in butter until they become translucent.

2. Add finely chopped garlic and one chopped potato along with a minced ripe red tomato.

3. Add chicken stock, bring to boil, then simmer on low heat until potatoes are tender.

4. Then add bunches of spinach and bring to boil a second time. Simmer for 5 minutes.

5. Season with salt and pepper.

6. Puree soup mixture in a blender and add a few spoonfuls of cream if you wish.

7. While the soup is cooking, in another pan, bring water to boil and cook eggs until the white and yolk is firm.

8. Peel shell off eggs and serve with warm soup.

*I often vary ingredients depending on what I feel like preparing as well as what is available and what I can afford at the time.*

*(Editors' note: It seems as if there are as many ways to boil eggs as there are people to boil them. Even if this is a bit of an exaggeration, the boiling methods do vary. Here you will find some sound advice about producing perfect hard boiled eggs: http://www.goodegg.com/boiledegg.html.)*

Mette Eliseussen is a tremendous campaigner against landmines and cluster bombs who helped found the national campaigns to ban landmines in Norway and in Afghanistan, where she lived from 1990-1997 as the Program Manager for Save the Children. With commitment and stamina to spare, Mette embarked with John Rodstad and others in a journey across the United States in 1997 to build support for the Mine Ban Treaty in the "Ban Bus." Eleven years later they did it again, this time across Europe in support of the 2008 Cluster Munition Convention that bans cluster bombs. You can see Mette and read John's "two minute history" of the ban bus at: http://thebanbus.org/the-ban-bus/. A sociologist by training, in addition to banning weapons, Mette has worked as a drug addict counselor, journalist, trauma counselor, publishing manager, and a mountain rescue specialist for over twenty years.

# DAWN ENGLE
# & IVAN SUVANJIEFF

*"Being a peace activist sometimes means putting 'the cause' before your family -- and when we created 'PEACEJAM,' a program designed to train a new generation of young leaders for peace work using the role model of Nobel Peace Laureates like Jody Williams, we soon found that we were constantly on the road. It was never ending travel, all over the USA and all around the world. Eventually, we simply decided to take our two teenage boys out of high school and to 'home school' them ourselves so that they could travel with us and we could do a better job as parents.*

*We became something akin to a circus family, traveling the world together -- and the boys quickly learned how to run every aspect of the program, from making name tags to running interactive workshops. What an incredible way for a family to bond! But we always missed being home. And whenever we finally DID get a couple of weeks home, it was just so special and sweet.*

*This recipe is for one of our 'celebration' meals -- we would make this whenever we got to spend some time together at home, sleeping in our own beds... and even though it is a very simple recipe that we picked up from a 60-minute gourmet type of book, really nothing fancy at all, making this meal always made us feel like we were on top of the world."*

## Chicken with Grapes & White Cream Sauce
### (Serves four)

Ingredients:

- 1¾ pounds skinless, boneless chicken breasts
- ½ cup fresh or canned seedless grapes
- 3 tablespoons butter
- 1½ tablespoons finely chopped shallots
- ½ cup dry white wine
- 1½ cups heavy cream
- Salt and freshly ground pepper to taste

*Preparation:*

1. Trim off all traces of fat, white membranes and so on from the chicken breasts. On a flat surface and using a flat mallet, pound them lightly. With a sharp knife, cut the breasts into half-inch strips. There should be about three cups.

2. If fresh grapes are available, remove the stems, then rinse and drain them well and set aside. If canned grapes are used, drain them and set aside.

3. Heat the butter in a large, heavy skillet and when very hot, but not brown, add the chicken breasts and sprinkle them with salt and pepper.

4. Cook over high heat, stirring constantly so that the pieces cook evenly and just until they lose their raw look and are barely cooked through, about 3 to 5 minutes.

5. Using a slotted spoon, transfer the chicken to a plate or shallow bowl and set aside.

6. Then add the shallots to the same skillet and cook briefly, stirring. Add the wine and continue cooking over high heat, shaking the skillet while stirring. As juices accumulate around the chicken pieces that have been set aside, pour them into the liquid cooking in the skillet. When the wine has cooked down by half, add the cream and continue cooking over high heat.

7. If using fresh grapes, add them now to the sauce. Cook over high heat about 4 to 5 minutes more or until the cream mixture takes on a sauce-like consistency. Add salt and pepper to taste.

8. If canned grapes are used, add them at the last minute of cooking, just to heat through.

9. Spoon the chicken back into the skillet with the sauce and heat through. Serve over rice.

*Curried rice is great with this dish!*

## About the Contributors...

Dawn Engle and Ivan Suvanjieff are a unique and indescribable pair who as friends and colleagues created the amazing non-governmental organization PeaceJam in 1996. In the process, they also got married – to each other. PeaceJam's mission is to create a new generation of leaders committed to positive change in themselves, their communities and the world through the inspiration of the work of Nobel Peace Laureates – and by spending time with individual Peace Laureates in youth leadership conferences in different locations around the world. The improbable duo – Dawn, once a button-down administrative chief for a Republican congressman, and Ivan, a wild man punk rocker and artist – are themselves inspiring examples of how you can take a fantastic idea and turn it into even more fantastic reality. Tens of thousands of young people have been part of the PeaceJam experience due to their creative vision – and much more importantly, their total commitment to turning that vision into the force for teaching peace that it is today. You can listen to Dawn and Ivan tell the story of the "Genesis of Peacejam" on a video at: www.peacejam.org/about.aspx/.

# EVE ENSLER

*"For the revolutionary on the go who is working to end war, stop the militarization of the planet, protect and empower women, honor the earth and indigenous people, and end racism and homophobia.*

*This recipe is quick, cheap, easy, and delish – and you don't have to know how to cook! It does not involve measurements. It is anarchic, creative, and based on intuition and love."*

## Activist Pasta

### Ingredients:

**Whole wheat penne pasta**
**Lots of garlic, chopped**
**Olive oil**
**Fresh basil, chopped**
**Fresh whole ripe tomatoes, chopped**

### Preparation:

1. Cook the pasta, but not too long: al dente.
2. Mix remaining ingredients, then pour over pasta.
3. Add salt to taste.

*Eat. Feed your friends. Feed the people.*

### About the Contributor...

Eve Ensler is a playwright, performer, feminist, and activist. She wrote the award-winning *Vagina Monologues*, which has been translated into 45 languages and performed in over 119 countries. Through her experiences with the play and its performances, she was inspired to create V-Day, a global movement to stop violence against women and girls. Eve Ensler is a force to be reckoned with who has taken her powerful words and put them to powerful action. Through annual benefit productions of Eve's plays, at last count, the V-Day movement had raised over $60 million and educated millions about the issue of violence towards women and the efforts to end it. Check it out at www.vday.org. And if you haven't done it yet, read *Vagina Monologues* and Eve Ensler's other work!

# SHIRIN ERSHADI

*"Here's a recipe for a healthy Persian summer dish or appetizer."*

## Persian Cucumber-Mint Yogurt

*Ingredients:*

**2 large salad cucumbers**
**4 cups low-fat or non-fat plain yogurt**
**Handful of red raisins**
**Handful of walnuts**
**Salt, pepper, dried mint**

*Preparation:*

1. Peel cucumbers and chop them into little pieces.
2. Add cucumbers, raisins and walnuts to yogurt; mix them all.
3. Add salt, pepper and dried mint to taste.
4. Refrigerate for an hour. Serve cool.
   *I hope you like it!*

*About the Contributor...*

Shirin Ershadi is attorney who lives in Los Angeles, where she is an interpreter; she also teaches and lectures on international law. Shirin Ershadi and Shirin Ebadi were students together in law school in Iran and have a long and close friendship. Ershadi often serves as interpreter for Shirin Ebadi and through that work has become an important friend of the Nobel Women's Initiative. Watching Shirin and Shirin joke and laugh together is a sight to behold. Shirin Ershadi is a committed advocate for the firm establishment of the International Criminal Court, created to try individuals for war crimes, genocide and crimes against humanity when they are able to evade justice in their own countries. She is a member of the International Criminal Court Alliance, a non-governmental organization based in California and founded to support the Court. For more information about the Alliance, please go to www.icc-alliance.org. For a picture of Shirin Ershadi and Shirin Ebadi together, check out: www.flickr.com/photos/43866215@N00/2413951897/.

# MIA
# FARROW

*"I used to make movies. And I acted in plays. I have fourteen kids, so between the kids and the career I was busy. Now that the kids are older, you'd think I'd be slowing down.*

*Actually, I never had a plan for this part of my life. But something happened that changed everything - big time. That 'something' is Darfur.*

*Since 2004, I have spent my days doing whatever I can think of to stop a genocide. It feels like head-banging most of the time, but I can't do anything else. I don't like traveling, but I do it a lot these days - about half the year. I go to eastern Chad, Sudan, CAR [Central African Republic] and around the USA trying to tell people what's happening in the Darfur region, and what we should all be doing about it. I started a website (www.miafarrow.org). My writing and my photos, taken over my ten trips into the region are there, and I blog most days. I write articles too.*

*The days aren't NEARLY long enough and I fall asleep thinking about the stuff I should have done. My dreams are crazy; I love them. And then it's morning… and this is where the pancakes come in. Honestly, apart from chocolate which I eat anytime and would happily replace ANY meal with, there is only one meal I really LOVE: breakfast… and it's all because of these pancakes. When I'm home, I make them every single morning. When I'm traveling, I miss them. They are the perfect food. I eat them with hot chocolate. This flawless combo sets me up just perfectly. I don't worry about the other meals, unless the kids are home."*

## Mia's Awesome Pancakes

*Ingredients:*

**2 egg whites OR 2 tablespoons vinegar**
**1 tablespoon olive oil**
**A dollop of apple sauce**
**A dollop of natural yogurt**
**¾ cup skim milk**
**1 cup whole wheat pancake mix**
**Oat bran (optional)**
**½ banana, mashed (optional)**
**Blueberries**
**Cinnamon to taste**

## Preparation:

1. Beat ingredients together, then fold in the blueberries.
2. Heat and grease pan.
3. Pour pancake mix onto pan into desired-size pancakes. Let rise.
4. Flip when golden brown on bottom.
5. Repeat until batter is gone.

*Enjoy! The vinegar alternative works just like eggs. It has no taste and it makes the pancakes rise better. Also, lately I've been adding cinnamon. It's supposed to be good for you.*

## About the Contributor...

Mia Farrow is not only a well-known actress, she's an activist driven by an intense commitment to help the people of Darfur, a region of Sudan that has been wracked by war since 2003. Named as an International Goodwill Ambassador for UNICEF in 2000, Mia began travel to Darfur on their behalf. She continues to travel to the region, although the Sudanese government now refuses her entry to Darfur, and has been countless times to Darfuri refugee camps in Chad and to witness the situation along with border with the Central African Republic. Mia talks fast, thinks faster, and has boundless energy and a hilarious sense of humor. A fierce advocate of the International Criminal Court, she very vocally support's the Court's issuance of an arrest warrant for Omar al-Bashir, Sudan's President, for crimes against his own people. Mia Farrow is a prolific blogger; you can find her at: www.miafarrow.org. For more information on the situation in Darfur, you can also check out: www.savedarfur.org.

# ALLISON
# FISHER

## Monday Night Post-Yoga Smoothie

*Ingredients:*

**1 frozen banana (this is a great way to use bananas that are starting to brown!)**
**1-2 cups vanilla soy milk**
**1-2 tablespoons creamy peanut butter**

*Preparation:*

1. Blend ingredients until desired consistency.
*Enjoy!*

*About the Contributor...*

Allison Fisher campaigns for safe energy and works for Public Citizen, a non-governmental organization (NGO) based in Washington, DC. She's been very involved in efforts by a coalition of NGOs to stop construction of a new nuclear reactor at the Calvert Cliffs Nuclear Power Plant in Maryland. The Calvert Cliffs site is the first attempt to build a nuclear reactor in the United States since such construction was halted more than three decades ago, after a nuclear accident at Three Mile Island near Harrisburg, Pennsylvania in 1979. Despite her protestations to the contrary, Allison isn't bad with a video camera either – she did a fine and efficient taping of a few comments from me for a citizen's hearing on Calvert Cliffs in 2008. Check out her work and see what you can do about safe energy at: www.citizen.org/action/. To see Alison Fisher testifying about Calvert Cliffs, go to: www.cepaonline.org/newsletter9.pdf.

# JESSICA GABRIAN

*"Fighting for what you believe in isn't always a walk in the park. When working toward Missouri's divestment from [companies doing business in] Darfur, there were plenty of people who did not think there was anything they could do to help. They did not see how the situation in Darfur could be alleviated with a little action from the middle of the USA. But what would the world be like if we stopped our work in the face of adversity? It's all the more reason to step up our game and find a new way to make our goal a success. I have found that sometimes all you need is a healthy meal and the company of good friends who believe in your cause and are ready to roll up their sleeves and climb on board. This 'Peace Bean Salad' is a perfect addition to a meal for getting the creative juices flowing. Serve and the ideas for action are soon to follow!"*

## Peace Bean Salad

### Ingredients:

**1 pound green beans**
**Olive oil**
**Canola oil**
**12 lemons**
**Full head of garlic, chopped into slices**
**Salt and pepper**

### Preparation:

1. Wash the beans and cut the ends off.
2. Blanch the beans: plunge them into boiling water for three minutes maximum, drain and immediately plunge into water with ice to stop the cooking. Drain again once cold and pat dry.
3. Put them in a bowl and cover with a mixture of half olive oil and half canola oil.
4. Squeeze the juice of 12 lemons over the beans.
5. Add garlic, salt and pepper.
6. Soak overnight until they taste good.
7. Drain the oil; eat just the beans.
   *Enjoy!*

## About the Contributor...

Jessica Gabrian "jams for peace" with PeaceJam, a non-governmental organization that connects determined youth with global peacemakers, focusing on Nobel Peace Prize Laureates. Jessica is one of the subjects of PeaceJam's "Simple Acts of Peace" documentary series, which is based on the Nobel Laureates' Global Call to Action – a call for young people to work to address ten areas that are causing the most suffering in the world, including Racism and Hate, the Spread of Global Disease, Access to Clean Water, and Rights for Women and their Role as Leaders. With her broad smile and open warmth and enthusiasm, Jessica Gabrian pretty easily convinces people to support her efforts for a better world. Outside of her volunteering for PeaceJam, Jessica's commitment to helping others took her to Washington, DC for graduate study at Gallaudet University, the world's leading university for the deaf and hard-of-hearing. She has become a fluent in American Sign Language. For more about Jessica Gabrian, read about her passion for helping others at: http://www.williamwoods.edu/ur/detail.asp?ID=1464/. Check out PeaceJam at: www.peacejam.org.

# EMILY GOOSE

*"A world of peace, happiness, and security. Who wouldn't want it? It's easy to say you want it, and think you want it... especially nowadays when the fad is to wear t-shirts with bold 70s-esque peace signs on them or sport bags that read "GO GREEN." But what does it really mean to advocate for peace?*

*We can think about peacemaking and how glorious our world would be if every child had access to clean water and three balanced meals a day, or if every wife or mother had the same rights as her husband, or father to the children she bore. We can ponder a serene place on earth where corrupt governments can't dominate society. Where innocent people aren't killed every day by weapons they never knew existed beneath the dirt on their playground or their route to work. Where people are educated enough to grasp what diseases mean and basic ways to cope with them. Where people who have more than anyone could ever want or need to survive decide to lend a helping hand to those less fortunate.*

*The fact is – our world is far from all of this and just the thought of how grand such a world would be won't bring us one. So what must we do? Take action. Seek everyday opportunities to help people, our environment, and our world. Get educated. Get involved. You'll find there are far more opportunities to do so than you may think.*

*To youth reading this: We are the foundation of the future. We must change the path that our world is headed in. How? Find something you're passionate about – more specific than 'peace.' What aspect of a peaceful world is most precious to your heart? What issue do you find yourself most attached to? And act on it. Take the world one step at a time. One person can't make a difference? This cookbook and its contributors are evidence: yes, you can."*

# Chocolate Mousse
# (& Cake)

*(Serves six)*

*Ingredients:*
- ¼ **cup sugar**
- ⅓ **cup water**
- 1½ **cups whipping cream**
- **16-ounce package semisweet chocolate pieces**
- **3 egg yolks**
- **3 tablespoons dark rum**
- ½ **cup almonds, toasted (optional)**

*Preparation:*

1. Combine sugar and water and bring to a boil. Boil for three minutes.

2. Whip whipping cream in Kitchen Aid, on speed 4 – gradually increase to speed 6. You could also use a metal blade (with plunger out) in a Cuisinart. Whip 60 seconds.

3. With chocolate pieces in Cuisinart using metal blade, chop with on-off motion for 15-20 seconds.

4. With the food processor on, pour the hot sugar/water mixture, egg yolks and dark rum through feed tube.

5. Add toasted almonds and run until just coarsely chopped.

6. Fold chocolate mixture gently into whipped cream.

7. Chill before serving.

8. You can turn this mousse into a **Mousse Cake** by lining a 9 x 5-inch jelly pan with store-bought ladyfingers. Place a row on each side and the bottom of the pan, with the inside of the fingers facing the inside of the pan. Pour half of mousse into pan. Place another row of lady fingers over the mousse. Pour the rest of the mousse into the pan. Place one final row of lady fingers to the top. Chill in refrigerator until serving time. Before serving, simply turn the pan upside down and pat until it comes loose.

*Enjoy!*

# Hollandaise Sauce

*Ingredients:*

**4 egg yolks**
**Juice of ½ large lemon**
**1½ cups butter, melted**
**¼ teaspoon cayenne pepper**

*Preparation:*

1. Place yolks into food processor.
2. Heat butter in microwave until boiling.
3. Turn on food processor and SLOWLY add the boiling butter. It is important to add the butter slowly so as not to curdle the eggs.
4. Add lemon juice and cayenne.
   *Enjoy!*

*About the Contributor...*

Emily Goose is a 2009 high school graduate from Fredericksburg Academy in Fredericksburg, Virginia and will begin college in September at Smith College – she'll be a terrific "Smithie," as the young women of Smith, an all-women's college, are called. She happens to be my stepdaughter and her father, whose recipes follow, is also a contributor to the cookbook, which Emily designed, laid out, and co-edited. She's warm, loving, fun and funny and realizes the critical state that much of our world is in and really, really wants to make a difference. Emily believes that this cookbook is proof that individuals can and will change the world. She has traveled to Honduras on community service trips to volunteer at orphanages there, attended PeaceJam conferences, and tries her hardest every day to do even the little things that make the world around her a better place. Emily Goose knows that today's youth are the foundation of tomorrow and those who know her have no doubt she will be a major force to change our world for the positive.

# STEPHEN
## GOOSE

*"Making food and making peace. Both are sometimes simple and sometimes complex. Both are a necessity for life but should also be seen as joyous undertakings. Both are best when they involve sharing and understanding. In whatever ways make sense in your particular circumstance, you should do both every day."*

## Sesame Beef

*Ingredients:*

    1 pound flank steak
    3 tablespoons sesame seeds, toasted
*For the Marinade:*
    ¼ cup soy sauce
    2 teaspoons honey
    1 tablespoon brown sugar
    1½ tablespoons dark sesame oil
    1 tablespoon fish sauce
    2 cloves garlic, minced (or more, to taste)
    10 twists ground black pepper (or more, to taste)
    1 pinch red pepper flakes (or more, to taste)
    2 scallions, chopped (optional)

*Preparation:*

1. Combine marinade ingredients (double if more than a pound of meat, good to have plenty of marinade).

2. Slice raw flank steak as thinly as possible, diagonally across the grain – this is KEY. It is easier to slice if meat is cold or even slightly frozen.

3. Put slices of meat into marinade for at least 30 minutes or up to several hours, turning occasionally.

4. Toast sesame seeds at 350°F for a couple of minutes – you must keep a close eye on them or they will burn. Add to marinade/beef and stir just before cooking.

5. Grill over medium-high heat. If sliced thin as called for, it will only take a couple of minutes per side. I sometimes find that by the time I have all the slices on the grill, it is time to start turning the first ones. You want a charred effect. After turning, splash with remaining marinade.

6. Remove from grill and serve.

# Goose's Fabulous BBQ Sauce

*Ingredients:*

**2 cups ketchup**
**5 tablespoons Worcestershire sauce**
**3 tablespoons A-1 sauce**
**3 tablespoons Heinz 57 sauce**
**2 tablespoons lemon juice**
**2-5 shakes Tabasco sauce**
**½ to ¾ teaspoon garlic powder**
**¾ teaspoon coarsely ground black pepper**
**¾ teaspoon seasoned salt**

*Preparation:*

1. Thoroughly mix together. You are looking for a bit of a tangy taste. Works with chicken, ribs, pork – an all-purpose BBQ sauce for grilling.

*(Editors' completely objective note: This BBQ sauce is outstanding! If you like to grill, you'll love this!)*

# Grilled Flank Steak Teriyaki

*(Serves four)*

*Ingredients:*

**1 pound flank steak**
*For the Marinade:*
**¼ cup oil**
**¼ cup soy sauce**
**2 tablespoons ketchup**
**1 tablespoon vinegar**
**2 tablespoons fish sauce**
**1 tablespoon sherry**
**1 teaspoon hoisin sauce**
**1 teaspoon minced ginger**
**2 cloves minced garlic (or more to taste)**
**2 shakes chili oil (or other hot sauce)**
**1 tablespoon cornstarch dissolved in water (just enough to dissolve it)**

*Preparation:*

1. Mix all the ingredients together. Marinade the flank steak at least one hour.

2. Grill over high heat approximately five minutes per side, depending on thickness of steak. You want the outside to be charred. After turning steak, splash some marinade on it; beware of flare up. Steak is best charred on outside, rare on the inside.

3. Carve and serve. Crucial: how you carve it. Slice as thin as you can, going diagonally against the grain of the steak. (Don't slice straight up and down.) Double marinade if using more than one pound of steak.

## Potatoes Gruyère
*(Serves four)*

*Ingredients:*

**8 medium to small red potatoes (peeled or unpeeled, as preferred), thinly sliced (Cuisinart – 4 mm blade is perfect.)**
**Salt substitute and pepper to taste**
**Minced garlic to taste**
**1-2 tablespoons flour per layer**
**Approximately ½ cup milk (or fat free half and half or heavy cream)**
**Paprika**

*Preparation:*

1. Preheat oven to 350°F.

2. Cook potatoes in already boiling water until still firm but not crunchy, check after 5 minutes. Drain.

3. Butter sides and bottom of a casserole dish.

4. Layer potatoes, so slices slightly overlap.

5. Sprinkle with salt substitute, pepper, and minced garlic (to taste); then light dusting of flour (approximately 1-2 tablespoons per layer); then cover layer with a layer of grated gruyere cheese. Repeat layers until no more potatoes are left.

6. On top layer, do not add flour, but make sure you add lots of cheese.

7. Pour milk over it all.

8. Sprinkle top with paprika.

9. Cover and bake for about 30 minutes.

10. Uncover and let top brown for 5-10 minutes. Crispy top and bubbling on the sides is desirable.

11. Remove and let come together for at least five minutes.

# Sautéed Green Beans with Garlic

*Ingredients:*

**Fresh green beans, 10-15 per person
1 clove of minced garlic per person
Butter & olive oil**

*Preparation:*

1. Slice off ends of beans diagonally. Plunge into boiling water for three minutes maximum, drain and immediately plunge into water with ice to stop the cooking. (This process, of course, is blanching.) You want the beans bright green and firm. Once beans are cooled, rinse again and set aside to dry on paper towel.

2. Heat enough butter and olive oil to cover bottom of sauté pan.

3. Add the garlic and beans. Sauté quickly on medium heat for 1-2 minutes. If desired, add salt, pepper, herbs de province.

4. Serve immediately.

*About the Contributor...*

Steve Goose is the director of Human Rights Watch's Arms Division. He has been fundamental in the banning of three weapons: blinding laser weapons in 1995, antipersonnel landmines in 1997, and cluster munitions in 2008, as well as the establishment of another international protocol in 2003 to try to address the humanitarian disaster of explosive remnants of war. He's often accused of being a lawyer and protests loudly that he's a (boring) researcher and not an activist. He most definitely could be a lawyer if he wished, he's a researcher although not boring at all, and is an activist par excellence. Unlike some other landmine campaigners, Steve Goose couldn't sing to save his soul and dances with a "White-boy overbite" but he is super fun, has a sharp, dry wit and can cook up a storm. Some of us also accuse him of brilliance, which he has more than exhibited in being, along with Canadian diplomat Bob Lawson, the intellectual architect of the Landmine Monitor, a ground-breaking civil society-led system of monitoring an international treaty – in this case the Mine Ban Treaty – which serves as a model for such monitoring. He and Human Rights Watch co-founded the International Campaign to Ban Landmines, which received the 1997 Nobel Peace Prize for the treaty that banned the use, production, stockpiling, and sale, transfer, or export of antipersonnel landmines. He and Human Rights Watch also co-founded the Cluster Munition Coalition, which was the engine that fueled the efforts to ban cluster munitions that resulted in the Cluster Munition Convention being successfully negotiated in 2008. As a final note, one of the editors of this cookbook is his daughter and the other is his wife, which might be one reason why this bio is a bit long – and we had to restrain ourselves from adding even more. Check out Goose and his work at: www.icbl.org and www.hrw.org and www.stopclustermunitions.org.

# PAUL HANNON
# & MAUREEN HOLLINGWORTH

*"On December 3, 2007, I was honored to host activists from around the world in Ottawa, Canada, to celebrate the 10th Anniversary of the Landmine Ban Treaty. On December 3, 2008, I [was] fortunate enough to be in Oslo, Norway, to help celebrate a new treaty banning cluster bombs. These treaties are vital steps in ensuring that innocent civilians are better protected from the rages of war. In both cases, these weapons were banned because individuals and organizations joined together to push governments to do the right thing. If we want a more peaceful world, it is up to each of us to do something about it. Clearly as civil society we can affect the change we want. So let's do it!"* Paul

*"I think of my own family history – how my grandparents were separated by WWI and how a generation later WWII affected the lives and plans of my parents, aunts and uncles. I think of other families around the world today separated by war and conflict, of people who have to flee their country to be safe, and of the perpetual insecurity of people who are internally displaced. While the term is used in many contexts (someone is 'at peace' or 'sleeping peacefully'), for me peace is not a state of mind; it is a state of being that is linked to the absence of war and conflict.*

*My maternal grandparents immigrated to Canada from the Isle of Man (between Ireland and England) in the second decade of the previous century – leaving a small island with declining mining prospects and few other employment opportunities for the chance of a better life in North America. They were actually engaged for about eleven years since my grandmother had to wait out WWI before being able to get passage on a boat to join my grandfather in Montreal. She traveled alone and married Grandpa a week after landing, having not seen him for six years.*

*This fruit sauce relish was a recipe she made in great quantities for the family every late summer when produce was fresh – along with many other preserves. I still make it annually, using my grandmother's handwritten and delightfully imprecise recipe as a guide and take along a jar when visiting members of that side of my family..."* Maureen

# Granny McGain's Fruit Sauce

*Ingredients:*

**10 ripe tomatoes**
**3 large apples**
**1 green pepper**
**2 onions**
**1 cup of sugar (brown or white)**
**2 teaspoons salt**
**1 cup cider vinegar**
**1 ounce "mixed spices," tied in cheesecloth; this is my version:**
**whole cloves, allspice, nutmeg, cinnamon and black peppercorns**

*Preparation:*

1. Chop and gently boil tomatoes, apples, green pepper and onions for 5-10 minutes.

2. Add sugar, salt, vinegar and spice bag.

3. Simmer with spice bag for about 1 hour.

4. Remove bag and continue simmering until mixture is thick and deep red in color.

5. Bottle in sterilized glass jars and seal.

6. If you wish, process in a boiling water bath for 15 minutes. Store jars in a cool, dark place. Once open, store in refrigerator.

*Fruit sauce makes a good companion for egg dishes and in grilled cheese sandwiches.*

*"Most of my family cooks and we all share a love of pickle relish and chutney. One summer in my early 20s, I joined my eldest cousin in Vermont for a pickle-making blitz. The following sweet relish was her way of using up an abundance of large garden zucchini (courgette). In the spirit of my grandmother, there is no standard recipe to follow, only guidelines. It is notable for being the one recipe in our household that Paul and I make together."* Maureen

## Granddaughters' Zucchini Relish

### Ingredients:

**Proportion of zucchini to other vegetables should be about 4:1.**
**About 8-10 cups green zucchini (leave skin on)**
**1-2 onions**
**1 green pepper**
**1 red pepper**
**Cider vinegar**
**1-2 cups brown sugar**
**1 tablespoon salt**
**Black peppercorn**
**Mustard seed**
**Whole allspice and cloves**
**1 cinnamon stick**

### Preparation:

1. Chop zucchini, onions and peppers into large chunks, then grind them up fine. We use manual grinder that clamps to the side of a counter or table. You could probably achieve the same result with much less effort using a food processor. Combine in a large pot and boil gently for 5-10 minutes.

2. Add enough cider vinegar to cover the ground up vegetables and then add brown sugar and salt.

3. In cheesecloth, tie the mix of black peppercorn, mustard seed, whole allspice and cloves, and add to the pot along with the cinnamon stick.

4. Simmer about one hour.

5. Bottle in sterilized glass jars and seal. If you wish, process in a boiling water bath for 15 minutes. Store jars in cool, dark place. Once open, store in refrigerator.

*This is a classic North American sweet relish used to top hamburgers or hot dogs... to give a little zip to an egg, tuna, salmon, chicken or turkey salad mix (for sandwiches)... or to make tartar sauce for fish.*

## About the Contributors...

Paul Hannon is the Executive Director of Mines Action Canada (MAC), a key non-governmental organization in the International Campaign to Ban Landmines (ICBL) and represents MAC on its Advisory Board. He is also on the Landmine Monitor Editorial Board and MAC serves as the lead NGO in getting the annual monster report (which hovers around 1,000 pages each year) to print. Paul is quite unassuming and on the surface may seem quiet, but he knows his mind and isn't afraid to share his views. He is a master of "process" and often helps keep the ICBL on an even keel. Paul and Maureen Hollingworth are life partners and their warmth and calm demeanors are in part the product of their years together. Maureen is a freelance editor and writer, with more than thirty years experience in international development, peace, and environmental issues. She has brought her writing and editing skills to the Landmine Monitor process in addition to all the other work she does. You'll find Mines Action Canada at: www.minesactioncanada.org and Paul in its Photo Gallery. Both Paul and Maureen are members of the steering committee of Ecology Ottawa, which works to promote citizen involvement in policies that affect Ottawa's environment. Check it out at: www.ecologyottawa.ca.

# PETER HERBY

*"[T]o be honest it is more Agneta's recipe than mine...I cook but more primitive stuff which would be unpublishable or cause indigestion." (Agneta Johannsen & Peter Herby are married.)*

## Saffron Chicken

*(Serves three to four)*

*Ingredients:*

**A tiny pinch of saffron powder** *(Editors' Note: We'd generally use a couple of threads of saffron)*
**2 teaspoons ground cinnamon**
**1 tablespoon paprika (sweet)**
**¼ teaspoon ground cloves**
**¼ teaspoon cayenne pepper**
**1 teaspoon salt**
**1 tablespoon ground ginger (powder)**
**1 tablespoon ground coriander (powder)**
**2 garlic cloves, minced**
**½ inch fresh ginger, grated**
**Fresh coriander, finely chopped**
**2 tablespoons lemon juice**
**3 tablespoons olive oil**
**4 chicken breast filets**
**5 tablespoons cream**
**Grape seed oil for frying**

*Preparation:*

1. Blend all ingredients except for the chicken and cream into a fairly thick paste.

2. Cut the chicken into bite-size pieces (or larger) and cover the chicken generously with the paste. Let stand for at least 5 minutes.

3. Heat grape seed oil in a frying pan and fry the chicken for 3 minutes on each side.

4. Transfer chicken onto plates and add the cream to the left over paste in the pan. Stir for a minute at high heat and pour sauce over chicken.

*Serve with couscous made with raisins, nuts, chicken broth and a little bit of salty butter, and green beans or courgettes (zucchini).*

Peter Herby is Coordinator of the Mines-Arms Unit in the Legal Division of the International Committee of the Red Cross (ICRC). Quiet on the surface, Peter brings fierce dedication and commitment to his work on weapons and international humanitarian law. He brought a wealth of experience to that work from his years with the Quaker Office at the United Nations in Geneva. The famously neutral ICRC took a bold stand in its call for a ban on antipersonnel landmines and its absolutely critical work to bring about the Mine Ban Treaty. Peter Herby has been a linchpin in that effort and more. He is one of a tiny few who has been fundamental in the banning of three weapons: blinding laser weapons in 1995, antipersonnel landmines in 1997, and cluster munitions in 2008, as well as the establishment of another international protocol in 2003 to try to address the humanitarian disaster of explosive remnants of war. Peter Herby may not himself be a good cook, but he's a terrific host. To find out more about Peter's work and the ICRC, please go to: www.icrc.org.

# FELICITY HILL

*"Anti-nuclear work isn't easy. You are working against the nightmare of nuclear war ever happening, as well nuclear waste that lasts 250,000 years; the magnitudes seem pretty overwhelming at times. That's why I started the Nuclear Free Salon (soon thereafter to be known as the No Nuke Saloon). The only people invited were confirmed plutonium head cases in New York. You know the type, we are the ones who talk about the CTBT on a Saturday night (that's the Comprehensive Test Ban Treaty) and who know the list of countries that have the 26,000 nuclear weapons in the world (that's the USA, Russia, the UK, France, China, India, Israel, Pakistan and North Korea) and we know in our hearts and souls that humanity will wake up from nuclear mistake. One night, I made lemon risotto and the group decided to form a religion around it. So I offer this peace recipe as a nuclear free inspiration."*

## Lemon Risotto

### Ingredients:

**Arborio rice**
**1 stock cube (some use chicken, I use veggie), dissolved in boiling water**
**1 large onion**
**1 stick of butter**
**1 block of parmesan cheese**
**Olive oil**
**Bottle of white wine (most of the alcohol cooks off)**
**1 large or 2 small lemons**
**Lemon thyme (optional, or use finely chopped parsley if unavailable)**

### Preparation:

1. In a very (very) healthy thwack of butter, (like half a stick of gorgeous melted butter); fry the finely chopped onion.

2. When the onion has caramelized, put the stove on medium heat.

3. Pour in about 2 cups of wine and 4-5 tablespoons of olive oil.

4. Throw in the rice - it should be under a little liquid.

5. Pour in some of the stock to cover it.

6. Stir. (Secret of risotto: keep stirring – never stop stirring!)

7. As the rice absorbs the liquid, pour some more wine in, little by little. Let it absorb the liquid and then pour in more stock. (You will get major glop issues if you pour in heaps of liquid and stir. It has to be little by little!)

8. Cover the rice in 3 millimeters depth of liquid and let it absorb.

9. Pour in more wine, let it absorb, let it absorb, keep stirring, pour more stock in.

10. About half way through, sprinkle in a handful of the grated Parmesan cheese - in total, sprinkle in about 3 handfuls.

11. When rice is nearly cooked, pour in the juice of 1 large or two small lemons (this is the secret of this recipe…).

12. Stir in the zest of the 1 large or 2 small lemons (i.e. the lemon skin, just the first two millimeters). (Yeah, I know you yanks don't have millimeters but get with the world—okay - join the century. Okay, okay, you're a friend, so it's the thickness of your thumbnail (very thin).)

13. Grate very gently with the part of the cheese grater you never use (the weird side with the little holes). That's for zest, (with maybe one or two strokes you get the zest off) and then move to another bit of the lemon.  It's important, which is why I'm going on about it. Stir the zest in at the very end.

14. Turn the heat off; let it sit for one minute with a nice thwack of butter on the top, melting by itself.  Stir it in to make it really delicious!

15. Dollop onto plates – sprinkle with some thyme or parsley to set it off.
   *Inhale!*

Felicity Hill, better known to those who love her as "Flick," is a major anti-nuke activist. She's currently working to stamp them out from Australia, where she works in the office of Senator Scott Ludlam of the Green Party. Flick is about as irreverent as they come and has a biting sense of humor – in case you couldn't tell from her recipe. Prior to her current work, Flick helped form the International Campaign to Abolish Nuclear Weapons. Flick also serves as the International Vice-President of the Women's International League for Peace a Freedom. WILPF is an international non-governmental organization (NGO) with national sections, covering all continents, with an international secretariat based in Geneva. WILPF is a storied organization formed in 1915 to empower women to work for peace and justice. In addition to holding an audience in the palm of her hand when she speaks, Felicity Hill is also a terrific and prolific writer. You can find about more about her and the organizations she works with at: www.wilpf.org and www.mapw.org. If you want to check out what she has to say about nuclear weapons and nuclear energy (bad), go to: www.vertic.org/assets/Felicity%20Hill%20presentation.pdf.

# MARK
## HIZNAY

*"After spending so much time in Geneva at fruitless multilateral disarmament negotiations in the past years, one of my favorite kitchen adventures is to make cheese fondue. Among some of my friends, this is a sacred process subject to much debate. Others could care less how it is made, but they eat it enthusiastically. If you want to sample a baseline cheese fondue, the packets of pre-made heat and serve fondue found in the deli/cheese section of a supermarket are actually not too bad, if not a little characterless. However, they must be imported from Switzerland.*

*There is, of course, never a right answer or consensus and I have tried to keep the [square brackets] to a minimum. The one thing guaranteed is that, like the Convention on Conventional Weapons, it will keep you coming back to Switzerland for years without a definite conclusion.*

*There are no required measurements for this recipe, just ingredients and personal taste preferences. You are striving for a smooth consistency at the end. You will need to adjust the amounts to the number of servings you are making. Except for Steve Goose who insists on drinking crappy beer from Geneva, the tradition is to serve cheese fondue with very cold Fendant (a dry Swiss white) wine. A dry white wine like a Sauvignon Blanc or Chenin Blanc will suffice. People who drink red wine with cheese fondue are deported to France. This recipe also assumes that you have an enamel fondue pot and burner set with a stand that includes a stove and fondue fuel for serving this at a table as well as those long forks, which are handy to stick in the back of certain pain in the ass delegates."*

## Cheese Fondue

Ingredients:
**Gruyère cheese**
**Emmanthal cheese**
**1 tablespoon of cornstarch**
**Wine**
**1 clove of garlic**
**A shot of Kirshwasser (cherry brandy)**
**Black pepper, freshly ground**
**¼ to ½ of a lemon's juice**
**French baguette**

# Preparation:

1. Grate equal amounts of both cheeses; mix them together. You may want to reserve some to correct for taste later in the process.

2. Mix cornstarch with some wine to make a smooth, but relatively thick, paste. Set aside, but remember to stir it before adding it later.

3. Crush garlic in a press. Rub paste onto the inside of the fondue pot, covering the entire interior.

4. Heat half a cup (or so) of wine over medium/medium-high heat until it begins to bubble.

5. Add Kirshwasser.

6. Add cheese, regulate heat to melt cheese at constant rate (be patient, do not let it burn) until all the cheese is added and is at a smooth consistency. Stir, stir, stir.

7. Grate in some nutmeg.

8. Add a few twists of black pepper from a mill.

9. Add lemon juice.

10. Keep the mixture over heat until it begins to bubble slowly but constantly. Did I mention, stir, stir, stir? If the oil in the cheese separates, you are probably using too much heat.

11. Get a piece of bread and taste your fondue. Adjust ingredient mix to taste. Stir, stir, stir. Repeat this process until you get what tastes good to you. Warning, people will get envious watching you doing such sampling. Don't worry if the fondue gets a little diluted some by adding additional wine/Kirshwasser.

12. When satisfied with the taste, slowly add amounts of the cornstarch/wine mixture until the fondue "binds," stirring all the time. Use your judgment on what binds means but add the cornstarch/wine mixture incrementally and let it take effect before adding more. If you keep stirring, you will feel it bind.

13. Remove from heat and place on the stand with a lit burner. Be careful to adjust the heat of the burner so as not to burn your fondue.

14. Serve with thickly cut cubes or slices of crusty baguette (we like to cut the bread and leave it out for a few hours). Encourage your guests to stir the fondue as they dip bread into it. If anyone makes the faux pas of losing their cube of bread from their long fork while they are dipping it in the fondue, that person must pay a penalty. Current practice is that they must drink whatever is in their wine glass or do a shot of Kirshwasser. This penalty is doubled for those who must drink beer with their fondue, like Steve Goose.

15. After everybody is full or the fondue is gone, scrape out the cheese "crust" from the bottom of the pot and watch the hard-core fondue-o-philes enjoy a real treat.

16. If you have a full belly and still have fondue left, pour the cheese onto a plate/bowl and refrigerate. It makes a yummy cheese omelet the next day!

*(Editors' Note: Leftover fondue is also great the next morning on a toasted bagel and put under broiler until it starts to bubble! For the discerning reader, it would appear that Hiznay and Goose duel over fondue! In any case, we will offer that in the Goose-Williams house, we don't bother with Kirshwasser, but we do also use some Havarti cheese in the cheese mix – it makes it creamier. We also toast our bread cubes in the oven and also serve baby potatoes, microwaved until tender, and pieces of broccoli, also microwaved but still crisp, to dip in the cheese. We believe in vegetables. I do, however, share Mr. Hiznay's distaste for beer with fondue. But then again, I think beer an unsuitable beverage any time.)*

## About the Contributor...

Mark Hiznay is a senior researcher with Human Rights Watch's Arms Division, where he works banning landmines and cluster bombs. Hiznay came to Human Rights Watch from the "dark side," having worked for years for a defense contractor in the Washington, DC area. Mark has a sharp eye, critical mind and withering sense of humor. He more than holds his own when debating the utility of weapons with military from countries around the world. Mark plays a key role in the annual production of the Landmine Monitor report. He has a penchant for sampling exotic beverages from various parts of our globe. Mark Hiznay is indispensable to the Arms Division, the International Campaign to Ban Landmines and the Cluster Munition Coalition. For more information, please go to: www.hrw.org or www.icbl.org or www.stopclustermunitions.org.

*(Editors' note: The CCW is an international treaty - the Convention on Conventional Weapons. It is, for the most part, a weak treaty that did little to eliminate the pain and suffering caused by landmines. The International Campaign to Ban Landmines tried to change the CCW so it would ban landmines, but it did not work. So, a completely new treaty -- the Mine Ban Treaty -- was negotiated separately and outside the UN. For more information about it all, go to: www.icbl.org. You also saw the term "square brackets." Square brackets are used in negotiating a treaty to indicate wording that has not yet been agreed upon. Once there is agreement on a word or phrase, the brackets are removed.)*

# BRIGID INDER

*"This salad is delicious. I was introduced to it by a great Sudanese activist and friend, Amira Khair. The first time we shared this salad was the night we spent monitoring the detention and torture of three Sudanese activists who had been illegally arrested by the government of Sudan. They were arrested because the government suspected they were cooperating with the International Criminal Court's investigation of the President in relation to the conflict in Darfur.*

*We knew the activists who had been detained and so the long night vigil of making phone calls and monitoring the internet was sustained by pizza (as you do!) and this salad. Eventually we received good news that two had been released, treated for their injuries and 'smuggled' out of Khartoum. One remained in custody but was also later released.*

*On 4 March 2009, the ICC issued an arrest warrant for President Al'Bashir of Sudan for war crimes and crimes against humanity. This is the first time the ICC had issued a warrant of arrest against a sitting Head of State.*

*It takes many different things to sustain our activism including of course good food and great friends. We are not sure whether President Al'Bashir likes this salad or not, but we are pretty sure it won't be served at the ICC Detention Centre in The Hague."*

## Sudanese Eggplant Salad
*(Serves four)*

### Ingredients:
**1 clove of Garlic**
**2-3 eggplants**
**1 large lemon**
**2 heaping spoonfuls of smooth peanut butter**
**½ cup non-flavored yogurt**
**1 large red capsicum (bell pepper)**
**2 medium sized carrots, diced**
**2-3 spoons vinegar**
**Salt and pepper to taste**
**¼ teaspoon raw garlic, chopped**

### Preparation:
1. Mix yogurt with peanut butter.
2. Add 2-3 pinches of salt (depending on taste and blood pressure); add pepper and garlic.
3. Add juice of lemon and, finally, vinegar.

4. Mix this into a paste.

5. Then, skin eggplants and slice finely (horizontally). Gently fry the eggplant circles. Once softened and lightly browned, take them off the heat and mash them up.

6. Cut capsicum into small pieces, along with carrots, and lightly sauté these together. Once ready (the carrots will still be slightly firm and crunchy), add this to the eggplant and mix.

7. Add mixture to the yogurt and peanut butter paste. Mix well; this is best done by hand.

*The salad can be eaten hot or cold and goes well with fish, chicken, couscous or even pizza. It can be eaten for lunch or dinner and as with most foods suitable for these meals, it will likely go well with a New Zealand Sauvignon Blanc, especially from the Marlborough and Central Otago regions.*

## About the Contributor...

Brigid Inder is the executive director of the Women's Initiatives for Gender Justice, which works around the world for justice for women and for an effective and independent International Criminal Court. Brigid's smile lights up her entire face – even as she's describing harrowing work to empower women in some of the worst combat zones in the world to strategize and struggle for their rightful places in peace processes and peace building as they also seek justice and support efforts to bring war criminals before the International Criminal Court. Brigid seems to be able to be in about five places at the same time and no matter where she is, she brings wisdom, humor and sharp analysis to the table. Find out more about Brigid Inder and the Women's Initiatives for Gender Justice at: www.iccwomen.org. For other work in support of the International Criminal Court, check out the website of the Coalition for an International Criminal Court at: www.iccnow.org. For information on the situation in Darfur, go to www.savedarfur.org.

# AIMEE JACHYM

## WEST MEETS EAST FUSION

*"I was stuck up in the mountains near the most heavily fortified portion of the DMZ [Demilitarized zone] in South Korea last January teaching English to Korean kids, whose fathers were all soldiers. Seven other American friends worked with me. I was the first foreigner many of them had ever met. I was making some mac and cheese for these friends, and someone asked if we had Tabasco. We did not have Tabasco, but the opportunity gave rise to cross-cultural fusion, which we shared with our kids and their parents on the last day of the winter camp. We couldn't tell whether their noses were running because of the spiciness of our food or the sub-zero temperatures outside."*

## Go-Chu Mac and Cheese

### Ingredients:

**Box of store-bought macaroni and cheese (Kraft or any other brand)**
**Milk**
**Butter**
**Go-chu-jang/Korean Red Pepper Paste (available at any Asian grocery store**

### Preparation:

1. Make a box of macaroni and cheese according to the directions on the back of the box. While still in the pot, mix in red pepper paste. If your nose doesn't run when you eat it, it's not spicy enough, and you need to add in more pepper paste. Approximately ¼ cup should do the trick for one box of mac and cheese.

*"Some KKOOM volunteers and I put on a Mexican Fiesta/Taco Party last year for the kids at an orphanage in South Korea. We thought that tacos would be a big hit, as our spaghetti dinner and other foreign food adventures were well-received in the past. However, perhaps not entirely to our surprise, many children forwent the tacos straight for the ice cream sundaes. The second biggest hit after the ice cream was the use of the leftover ingredients the next day, when one of the orphanage "aunts" (staff members)-- having never before tried Mexican food--cooked up some impromptu kimchi quesadillas."*

# Kimchi Quesadillas

## Ingredients:

**Flour tortillas**
**Shredded cheese (e.g., cheddar or Monterey Jack)**
**Kimchi/Korean Pickled Cabbage (available at your local grocery store in a jar in the produce section or at a Korean grocery store)**
**Oil/butter**

## Preparation:

1. Drain the water out of the kimchi.

2. Brown the kimchi by placing it in a small skillet over medium-high heat, turning to cook both sides. When kimchi is slightly brown on both sides, remove it from the pan.

3. Heat the medium-sized skillet to medium-high and add a small amount of oil or butter to grease the pan.

4. Place one large flour tortilla in the pan. Flip the tortilla over a few times, 10 seconds between flips. Air pockets should form within the tortilla.

5. When pockets of air begin to form, sprinkle a handful of shredded cheese over the top of the tortilla. Add the browned kimchi until the cheese is completely covered.

6. Reduce the heat to low and cover the pan. If it begins to smoke, remove the pan from heat. After a minute, check to see if the cheese is melted. If not, return the cover, wait another minute, and check again. When the cheese is sufficiently melted, use a spatula to lift up one side of the quesadilla and fold it over in half. The bottom of the quesadilla should by now be browned slightly. If it is not, turn the heat up to high and flip the quesadilla over every 10 seconds or so until it browns. Remove from pan and cut into wedges.

## About the Contributor...

Aimee Jachym was a PeaceJam mentor when we first met at a PeaceJam conference in Kalamazoo, Michigan. As a result of that conference we became e-pals and have kept in regular email communication ever since. After university, Aimee went to South Korea, where she was born, as a Fulbright Scholar and while there started volunteering at an orphanage. One thing led to another and in 2007, she founded Korean Kids & Orphanage Outreach Mission – KKOOM, a not-for-profit organization to help kids in orphanages in South Korea as well as to aid the institutions themselves and the staff who devote their time and resources to raising these kids. Aimee is an amazing and wonderful young woman who also happens to be an attorney. For more on her work, please go to: www.KKOOM.org.

# ANTONIA JUHASZ

*"As a writer and an activist armed with my own laptop and internet connection, my life can become incredibly isolated. Many of us take it as a badge of honor that we are simply too busy to take time off for ourselves or to enjoy those around us. We must constantly resist the urge to do so. Cooking and eating together are uniquely warm experiences that allow for a type of shared intimacy that is crucial for those of us struggling together against the evil in the world.*

*As an anti-war activist, I spend much of my time looking for, uncovering, cataloguing, and sharing the most criminal acts that the world has to offer. My new book,* The Tyranny of Oil: the World's Most Powerful Industry—and What We Must Do To Stop It, *brought me even more fully into the lion's den of Big Oil, global warming and wars for the most mundane reasons possible: greed and power. Fortunately, I work with people and with organizations that want to do something about all of this: the Institute for Policy Studies and Oil Change International.*

*And fortunately, I have found a book,* Two Dollar Dinners, *by Paul Gayler, that allows me to share the joy of cooking with my friends and fellow activists in a way that is easy enough that even I can make it. I have also found that soup brings people together better than just about any type of food. Here's my favorite recipe from the book. Cook it, share it and enjoy it with as many people as possible!"*

## Roasted Corn Broth with Chunky Pea Guacamole

*Ingredients:*

*Roasted Corn Broth:*
   **3 ears of corn**
   **4 tablespoons butter, melted**
   **Salt and freshly ground pepper**
   **2½ cups chicken or vegetable broth**
   **1½ cups cooked black beans**
   **½ cup cheddar cheese, coarsely shredded**
*Chunky Pea Guacamole:*
   **1½ cups cooked peas**
   **1 small green chili pepper, halved, de-seeded, and finely chopped**
   **3 tablespoons fresh cilantro, chopped**
   **3 tablespoons scallions, finely chopped**
   **2 tomatoes, de-seeded and cut into small pieces**
   **1 teaspoon fresh lime juice**

## Preparation:

*Roasted Corn Broth:*

1. Preheat oven to 400°F.

2. Put the ears of corn on a baking sheet, brush with the butter, sprinkle with salt and pepper, and cook until tender and lightly browned; this will take 20-25 minutes. Turn the corn regularly so they brown evenly.

3. Remove from the oven and when cool enough to handle, hold the corn over a chopping board and use a knife to scrape off all the kernels; reserve the kernels. Cut the cobs into chunks and return to the oven to roast for another 10 minutes.

4. Bring the broth to a boil in a saucepan. Add the roasted cobs, reduce the heat, and simmer for 40-45 minutes.

5. Strain the corn broth through a strainer and season to taste.

*Chunky Pea Guacamole:*

6. Mash the peas with a fork; add the remaining ingredients; season to taste.

7. To serve, divide the guacamole between four soup plates or bowls, add the reserved corn kernels and the black beans, then add broth to each bowl and top with shredded cheese.

8. Serve at once.

## About the Contributor...

Antonia Juhasz is a writer, political activist, speaker and teacher. One of the many things she is doing now is serving as director of the newly-established "Chevron Program" at Global Exchange, a human rights non-governmental organization in San Francisco, California. Her most recent books are *The Bush Agenda: Invading the World One Economy at a Time* and *The Tyranny of Oil: the World's Most Powerful Industry and What We Must Do To Stop It.* Antonia can take the most complex and threatening sounding issues and make them clear and understandable. She also makes clear and understandable what we can do to make things better for our world. If you've not read her books, you should. If you've never heard her speak, rush to the closest place she's giving a talk a listen! For more information about Antonia Juhasz and her work, check out: www.tyrannyofoil.org. See also: www.globalexchange.org.

# CELE
# KEEPER

*"The family had a bay house in La Porte, Texas where every Sunday for a house full of friends and relatives, Erna produced her magnificent gumbo. Erna died in 1949. This represents a fond memory from my childhood. The parentheses along the way were added by me, Erna's daughter."*

## Erna Sass's Seafood Gumbo
*(Makes about a gallon)*

*Ingredients:*

6 tablespoons shortening (I use olive oil)
6 tablespoons flour
6 cloves garlic, finely chopped
½ green onion, finely chopped
½ bell pepper, finely chopped
½ cup celery, finely chopped
¼ bunch parsley, finely chopped
2 cups fresh tomatoes, finely diced (I use canned, peeled tomatoes)
1 pound fresh okra, sliced into ¼ inch slices (I use packaged frozen okra, sliced)
3 quarts water
3 bay leaves
½ teaspoon thyme
1 teaspoon file (pronounced "feel-lay") powder
2 teaspoons salt
½ teaspoon black pepper
Dash of Tabasco
Dash of red pepper
Dash of Worcestershire sauce
2 pounds raw, peeled shrimp
1 dozen cooked crab claws and bodies (Only full, blue-bodied crabs need apply. You could use fresh crabmeat, but that would be wrong!)
1 pint raw oysters with juice (if desired)

## Preparation:

1. Prepare the roux: In a heavy cast-iron pot over low heat, add oil. Add flour slowly, stirring CONSTANTLY to avoid lumps and sticking until roux is medium brown color.

2. Add chopped garlic, onions, celery, bell pepper and parsley, then stir to blend in all these new additions. (Remember, you're still stirring.)

3. Add all seasonings except Tabasco and Worcestershire. Add tomatoes, then water, a little at a time, blending. (Are we stirring?) Bring to a boil, still stirring. Reduce to LOW heat, cover and simmer 2-3 hours. Stir. Occasionally check for sticking.

4. After cooking one hour, add the okra. Stir well and continue cooking. In the last 20 minutes, add peeled raw shrimp, crab bodies and claws. Add oysters (if desired). Stir well. Begin tasting for desired flavor. Fiddle with seasonings. Use the Tabasco and the Worcestershire sauces now, if you wish. Simmer at least 30 more minutes.

*Serve gumbo in soup bowls over cooked rice. Bring the Tabasco to the table. Have saltines and/or French baguettes. If you can't stand the garlic, get out of the kitchen. (Apologies to Pres. Harry S. Truman)*

## About the Contributor...

Cele Keeper is one hell of a woman. She's in her early 80s but you'd never know it. Sharp as a tack and funny as they come, Cele does more in a week than many of us do in a lifetime. She's a fierce political activist in her native Texas and a generous philanthropist. Cele and Sam, her husband, have endowed a professorship at the University of Houston's Graduate College of Social Work. Every now and then she and Sam escape to New York where they see every play they can and don't sleep for a week.

# COLLEEN KELLY

"The story behind Mrs. Thrasher's apple pie goes like this: When I was in nursing school, a very kind couple - the Thrashers, let me 'house sit' for them from November to May. Mrs. Thrasher's health required that she escape the harsh Northeast winter to Arizona for a few months. In return for bringing in the mail, I received free room (house really). Mrs. Thrasher was also a culinary wiz and she would often invite me to join them for meals during the times we overlapped at the house. By graduation, Mrs. Thrasher had given me her award winning apple pie recipe, which I have used fervently - winning hearts and stomachs over the years.

My brother Bill also became interested in the recipe. He had developed a love of cooking, and from the minute he first had Mrs. Thrasher's pie, it became 'his.' From then on, Bill made Mrs. Thrasher's apple pie every Thanksgiving - his favorite holiday. Bill was killed on 9-11 in the Towers he never even worked at.

I now make Mrs. Thrasher's apple pie every Thanksgiving. It's not only a way to memorialize Bill, but also to teach my children a bit more about his character. He gave thanks. He was kind. He was eclectic and interested in lots of things.

On the day of March 19th, 2003 I felt compelled to bake. But apple pie didn't feel right. Months of intense anti-war work was failing. In solidarity with Iraqi women I made bread and cried and tried to imagine what it might be like for them in the coming days when the U.S. would surely begin its bombing campaign. Yes, I made bread, a staple of life, not apple pie. In a political environment trying its hardest to connect Saddam with 9-11, I was not willing to have even two degrees of separation. I would not connect my brother Bill - the apple pie guy -with the beginning of the Iraq war. But every Thanksgiving I still bake apple pie ... and remember."

## Mrs. Thrasher's Apple Pie

Ingredients:

Crust:

**2 cups flour**
**1 teaspoon salt**
**⅔ cup plus 2 tablespoons shortening**
**¼ cup cold water (I use an ice cube, then remove before adding!)**
**Mix ingredients together. Chill in refrigerator for 30 minutes. Roll out.**

*Filling:*

**1 cup raisins, soaked in warm water and drained**
**¾ cup sugar**
**1 tablespoon flour**
**1 teaspoon cinnamon**
**1-2 tablespoons lemon juice**
**2 tablespoons sweet butter**
**1 egg, beaten together with 1 tablespoon cream**
**6 Granny Smith or Cortland apples (the tartness a must!)**

## Preparation:

1.  Preheat oven to 450°F.

2. Combine sugar, flour and cinnamon (the sugar mixture).

3. Slice peeled apples; sprinkle with lemon juice, and dust with ½ cup of the sugar mixture.

4. Add raisins. Scatter remaining sugar mixture on bottom crust.

5. Layer apple/raisin mix in crust. Dot with butter.

6. Lay on top crust, crimp, then brush on thin egg glaze.

7. Dot crow's feet around eyes with leftover egg glaze (prevents wrinkles).

8. Bake for 10 minutes at 450°F then 40 minutes at 350°F.

*Experience throughout the years with healthier substitutions and proportions.*

## About the Contributor...

Colleen Kelly is one of the founders of the "September Eleventh Families for Peaceful Tomorrows." They describe themselves best: "Peaceful Tomorrows is an organization founded by family members of those killed on September 11th who have united to turn our grief into action for peace. By developing and advocating nonviolent options and actions in the pursuit of justice, we hope to break the cycles of violence engendered by war and terrorism. Acknowledging our common experience with all people affected by violence throughout the world, we work to create a safer and more peaceful world for everyone." Colleen and others from Peaceful Tomorrows inspire me to try to be a better person. The desire for revenge is an understandable emotion; the ability to overcome that emotion and work for peace and justice is truly awe-inspiring. We all have a lot to learn from people like Colleen Kelly (or Robi Damelin, also a recipe contributor). For more on Colleen and Peaceful Tomorrows, please go to: www.peacefultomorrows.org. You'll find Colleen Kelly there at:
www.peacefultomorrows.org/article.php?list=type&type=48.

# REVEREND DR.
## REBECCA LARSON

*"This is an exceptionally easy recipe but it is the one that I get asked for more often than any other. I think the reason is the warm rich and 'cozy' fragrance that fills the house and the delicious hot taste on a cold winter night."*

## Winter Wassail

*Ingredients:*

> **6 cups apple cider or juice**
> **1 cinnamon stick**
> **¼ teaspoon nutmeg**
> **¼ cup honey**
> **3 tablespoons lemon juice**
> **1 teaspoon grated lemon peel**
> **1 18-ounce can unsweetened pineapple juice**
> **1 orange for Orange Stars (below)**
> **Cinnamon sticks**

*Preparation:*

1. In large saucepan, bring cider and one cinnamon stick to a boil; reduce heat. Cover; simmer 5 minutes.

2. Uncover; stir in remaining ingredients except Orange Stars and cinnamon sticks and simmer 5 minutes longer.

3. Create Orange Stars: Cut an orange into ¼ inch slices. Insert 5 whole cloves at equal intervals on the edge of each slice. Cut out a wedge of peel and pulp between each 2 cloves.

4. Serve in punch bowl; float Orange Stars in bowl.

5. Use cinnamon sticks as individual stirrers.

## About the Contributor...

Rev. Dr. Rebecca Larson is currently the executive director of the Division for Church in Society of the Evangelical Lutheran Church in America (ELCA), in Chicago, Illinois. Before that, Rebecca lived with her family for many years in Geneva, Switzerland, where she worked for the Lutheran World Federation and represented LWF in the International Campaign to Ban Landmines (ICBL). Rebecca's deep wisdom and even temper often helped to calm somewhat "passionate" discussions on policy or strategy in the ICBL. Her work at ECLA covers development education, public policy advocacy, disaster response, and policy development. She has led the federation's education efforts on topics like poverty, international debt, humanitarian intervention in complex emergencies, and HIV/AIDS. The "Rev. Doc" officiated at the wedding ceremony of contributors Williams and Goose at the Lutheran Church in Geneva, Switzerland, where her husband Stephen was serving as pastor. Find out more about Rebecca Larson and what she does at: www.elca.org.

# LIEUTENANT-GOVERNOR BARBARA LAWTON

*"Our cuisine reflects the history of our culture and land, but also opens up to broader definition with each new food and spice introduced into the vernacular. I see, in our evolving diets and in the very intimate act of breaking bread together, the promise of understanding and peace.*

*Fresh figs are not easy to come by in northern WI but when I have them, this is my idea of heaven."*

Special equipment: this dessert recipe requires an 11¼x8x1-inch rectangular or a 10-inch round fluted tart pan, one-inch deep, with a removable bottom.

## Fresh Fig Tart with Rosemary Cornmeal Crust and Lemon Mascarpone Cream

*Ingredients:*

Crust:

- 1½ cups all-purpose flour
- ½ cup yellow cornmeal (not stone-ground)
- 1 tablespoon sugar
- ¼ teaspoon salt
- 1 stick (½ cup) cold unsalted butter, cut into pieces
- 1½ tablespoons fresh rosemary, finely chopped
- 4-5 tablespoons ice water

Filling:

- ⅓ cup sour cream
- 1 cup mascarpone cheese
- ¼ cup sugar
- 1½ teaspoons finely grated fresh lemon zest
- ⅛ teaspoon salt
- 2 tablespoons red-currant jelly
- 1 tablespoon honey
- 1½ pounds fresh figs

*Preparation:*

Crust:

1. Preheat oven to 400°F.

2. Pulse together flour, cornmeal, sugar, and salt in a food processor. dd butter and rosemary; pulse until mixture resembles coarse meal with some mall (roughly pea-size) butter lumps. Drizzle evenly with 4 tablespoons ice ater and pulse until just incorporated.

3.  Gently squeeze a small handful: if it doesn't hold together, add more water, ½ tablespoon at a time, pulsing after each addition and continuing to test.

4.  Press dough evenly onto bottom and sides of tart pan with floured fingers. Smooth dough with a small offset metal spatula or back of a spoon (floured if necessary), then roll a rolling pin over top of pan to trim the dough overflowing the rim. Chill crust until firm, about 30 minutes.

5.  Bake crust in middle of oven until center and edges are golden, 25 to 30 minutes (don't worry if bottom of crust cracks), then cool in pan on a rack.

*Filling & Assemble Tart:*

6.  Whisk together sour cream, mascarpone, sugar, zest and salt in a bowl.

7.  Heat jelly and honey in a small saucepan over moderately low heat, whisking, until jelly is melted, about 4 minutes, then cool glaze slightly.

8.  Remove side of tart pan and spread mascarpone cream in shell. Cut figs lengthwise into ¼ inch thick slices and arrange decoratively over cream. Brush figs with honey glaze.

*(Notes: Crust can be made one day ahead and kept, covered, at room temperature. Mascarpone mixture can be made one day ahead and chilled, covered. Tart can be assembled one hour ahead and kept, loosely covered, at room temperature.)*

*(Editors' Note: This favorite recipe of Barbara Lawton's is found on www.Epicurious.com.)*

## About the Contributor...

Barbara Lawton is the Lieutenant-Governor of Wisconsin, a member of the Democratic Party, and became the first woman elected to this position in 2002; she was re-elected in 2006. The "Green Lieutenant-Governor," Barbara Lawton has taken on many issues related to economic development, climate change and clean energy policy. She's also a leading advocate for women in the workplace. Barbara has a dazzling smile, infectious sense of humor and is really fun to talk with about issues from the mundane to the extremely complex. Even as she is helping manage the great state of Wisconsin on the shores of the Great Lakes and coordinating climate change efforts in the Mid-West, she's also a great friend of the Nobel Women's Initiative and has brought her expertise to various NWI activities. We are both "Ambassadors" for Oxfam's climate change initative, "Sisters on the Planet." For a wealth of information on Lt.-Governor Barbara Lawton, go to: ltgov.wisconsin.gov. Also check out: www.oxfamamerica.org/campaigns/climate-change/sisters-on-the-planet/.

# NANG LAO LIANG WON (TAY TAY)

*"During my very first few years staying out of my country, Burma, I naturally missed home and missed the food. At that time, I did not really know how to cook (meaning I was not 'a proper woman' in the context of culture in Burma, where women are expected to learn how to cook well). I asked some friends from Burma and tried to learn to cook some Burmese dishes. My neighbors and friends, most of who come from different countries, were very supportive. They were the main tasters of my cooking, giving warmth, friendship and moral support to me all along. We would talk about the situation in Burma over meals."*

## Coconut Rice

### Ingredients:

- **1 cup coconut milk**
- **1 large red shallot, shredded**
- **3 cups of uncooked rice**
- **Salt to taste**

### Preparation:

1. Rinse the rice and put all the ingredients in the pot (with a pinch of salt if you like).

2. Stir briefly to make sure all ingredients are evenly mixed.

3. Add water until it is about 1 centimeter above the rice. Stir briefly again when it starts to boil, then simmer it until rice is tender and liquid absorbed.

## Chicken Curry

### Ingredients:

- **6 pieces chicken (drumstick or breast)**
- **3 tablespoons soybean oil**
- **A pinch of turmeric powder for chicken**
- **A pinch of red pepper (if you like it a bit spicy)**
- **6 large red shallots, finely chopped**
- **Salt to taste**
- **2 teaspoons fish sauce (optional)**

*Preparation:*

1.  Rinse the chicken and mix with turmeric powder, red pepper, and salt (and optional fish sauce, if you decide to use it); marinade it for a few minutes.

2. Meanwhile, fry the chopped red shallots, sprinkled with a pinch of turmeric powder and red pepper on low heat until they become soft.

3. Add the chicken with all the marinating juice and stir. Cook at a very low heat; simmer until chicken is soft enough and curry becomes oily. You can add a bit of hot water if the chicken is not cooked enough. You can also prepare a shallot salad (Burmese style) to go with this dish.

## Burmese-Style Shallot Salad

*Ingredients:*

**2 large shallots, chopped**
**Green chilies (depending on how spicy you want it)**
**Fresh lemon juice (or clear vinegar)**
**Fresh mint**

*Preparation:*

1.  Combine shallots, chilies, and lemon juice. Then sprinkle with mint.

*In Burma, traditional Burmese food is cooked at home, and served at most social functions. Nowadays it is also available at restaurants.*

*About the Contributor...*

Nang Lao Liang Won, also known as Tay Tay, is a women's rights activist and member of the Shan Women's Action Network, one of the eleven member organizations of the Women's League of Burma (WLB). The WLB's member groups have come together to "increase the participation of women in the struggle for democracy and human rights, to build mutual understanding among all nationals and participate in the national reconciliation and development process, and to enhance the role of the women of Burma both at national and international levels…" Tay Tay is a feminist activist and is a clear and forceful advocate for not only Shan women, but all women of Burma. She works tirelessly to bring freedom to her people. Please go to www.womenofburma.org to learn a wealth of information about the WLB, its member organizations, and their efforts to bring peace and democracy to the peoples of Burma. And once you are at the Women's League of Burma website, you will find a wealth of information on the situation in Burma by clicking onto "links" in the menu bar on the site.

# PROFESSOR
# WANGARI MAATHAI

## Stewed Spinach & Amaranth

*Ingredients:*

**1 tablespoon olive oil**
**2 tomatoes, chopped**
**1 onion, chopped**
**1 bunch of spinach, chopped**
**1 bunch of amaranth leaves, chopped**
**½ bouillon cube**

*Preparation:*

1. Heat the oil in a sauce pan and sauté the onion. Once translucent or lightly brown add the tomatoes.

2. Once the tomatoes have become a thick sauce, lower the heat and break the bouillon cube into the sauce and mix in.

3. Mix the chopped spinach and amaranth leaves and add to the sauce.

4. Stir in to coat the vegetables with the sauce.

5. Add a few tablespoons of water to steam the vegetables. Steam until vegetables are cooked.

*(Editors' Note: Amaranth is a genus of herbs; people around the world value amaranths as leaf vegetables.)*

## Mataha
## (Red Beans, Corn and Potatoes)

*Ingredients:*

**½ pound dried red beans**
**1 pound white corn, off the cob**
**8 medium potatoes, peeled and cut into large cubes**
**10 pumpkin leaves, coarsely chopped**
**Salt to taste**

## Preparation:

1. Soak the beans and maize overnight in water to cover.
2. Drain; cover again with water; add salt to taste, and boil gently for 2½ hours or until soft.
3. Drain and set aside.
4. Cover potatoes with water and boil until nearly soft.
5. Add pumpkin leaves and cook until tender.
6. Add maize and beans to the potatoes and pumpkin leaves and mash together.
7. The mixture should be dense and firm.
8. Adjust salt to taste as needed.

*Serve with chicken or beef stew.*


## About the Contributor...

Dr. Wangari Maathai is an environmental and political activist and in 2004, she became the first African woman to receive the Nobel Peace Prize for her contributions to sustainable development, democracy, and peace. She founded the Greenbelt Movement, which focuses on environmental conservation/tree planting, civic and environmental education, women for change, international advocacy for the environment, good governance, equity and cultures of peace. Wangari's smile is as big as her heart and her commitment to environmental justice, the empowerment of women and girls and good government for all. It was over tea in Nairobi with Wangari Maathai, Shirin Ebadi and Jody Williams at the end of 2004 that the idea of the Nobel Women's Initiative was born. Wangari has been a member of Parliament and served as Assistant Minister for Environment and Natural Resources in the government of Kenya. She is the author of *The Challenge for Africa, Unbowed,* and *The Green Belt Movement.* Please go to www.greenbeltmovement.org, for more information about Dr. Wangari Maathai.

# MAIREAD MAGUIRE

*"I love this recipe and I hope that sharing it with others will bring them the same enjoyment — both cooking and eating it with friends and family."*

## Pavlova

### Ingredients:

**10 egg whites – room temperature**
**1 cup castor sugar (super fine sugar)**
**2 teaspoons vinegar**
**2 teaspoons corn flour (corn starch)**
**1 pint double cream (if not available, use heavy cream/whipping cream)**
**Strawberries for decoration (or mixture of favorite fruits and chocolate flakes)**

### Preparation:

1. Preheat oven to 350°F.
2. Line large flat baking sheet with parchment paper.
3. Mix eggs in mixer on high until tripled size.
4. Slowly add sugar and continue mixing until meringue is stiff.
5. Add corn flour and mix for 2 minutes.
6. Add vinegar and mix for 2 minutes.
7. Transfer mixture onto greaseproof paper and pile high about 10 centimeters round.
8. Cook in oven about 20 minutes until light brown and cracks have appeared.
9. Remove from oven and leave in warm room for 20 minutes; then turn onto a plate and wait until cold.
10. Decorate with whipped cream and fruit of choice.

*From Ireland – via Russia – with love…*

*(Editors' Note: For commentary on "Pavlova," see contribution from Mary Wareham.)*

Mairead Maguire was the co-founder of the Community of Peace People, an organization founded to encourage a peaceful resolution of the "troubles" in Northern Ireland. For her work, she received the Nobel Peace Prize in 1976, along with the organization's co-founder Betty Williams. Recognized the world over for her campaigning for human rights, Mairead Maguire is firmly committed to the principles of non-violent action for political change. But one should never underestimate the power behind her kind, broad smile and soft-spoken approach to justice. She is tireless and relentless in her desire for a just world. She has been tear-gassed, shot with rubber bullets and arrested and deported – all for her work for the people of Palestine. Mairead is a member of the Nobel Women's Initiative. For more about Mairead Maguire and her work, please go to: www.peacepeople.com.

# CONGRESSMAN JIM MCGOVERN

## Aunt Jerry McGovern's Guiness Stew
*(Serves six)*

*Ingredients:*

**3 tablespoons olive oil**
**2 bay leaves**
**3 pounds beef chuck, cubed**
**2 onions, chopped**
**2 tablespoons flour**
**1 12-ounce bottle of Guiness**
**1½ to 2 cups beef stock**
**1 pound carrots, peeled and cubed**
**1 pound parsnips, peeled and cubed**
**1 tablespoon parsley, chopped**
**¾ cup dried prunes, finely chopped**
**1 small rutabaga, cubed**
**Salt and pepper to taste**

*Preparation:*

1. Preheat oven to 300°F.

2. Heat oil in large, heavy pan. Add bay leaves to heated oil and cook until they crackle. Remove from pan.

3. Brown meat in batches and set aside.

4. Cook onions until translucent and return beef to pan. Sprinkle meat and onions with flour and cook several minutes until flour begins to brown.

5. Add Guinness and beef broth to cover. Bring meat mixture to boil on top of stove. Cover and place in oven for one hour.

6. Add vegetables and prunes and cook an additional hour.

7. Test vegetables for tenderness.

8. Add parsley, salt, and pepper.

9. If broth seems thin, thicken with a few tablespoons of corn starch dissolved in beef stock.

*The stew tastes even better if made a day ahead!*

Jim McGovern has been a Democratic member of the US House of Representatives from Massachusetts since 1997; he's now serving his seventh term in office. Jim is committed to creating a better world, not only for his constituents in Massachusetts, but also for people everywhere. He is a human rights champion and a personal hero ever since we first met and he saved my skin more than once when I was working to stop US involvement in El Salvador in the 1980s. Jim McGovern is a great human being who puts good back into the word "politician." For more about Congressman Jim McGovern, please go to: http://mcgovern.house.gov/.

# MARY ELLEN MCNISH

*"Here is a Brunch Casserole that is guaranteed to bring peace to the world!"*

## Brunch Casserole

*Ingredients:*

**4 cups day-old French bread, cubed**
**1 teaspoon salt**
**2 cups cheddar cheese, shredded**
**¼ teaspoon onion powder**
**10 eggs, slightly beaten**
**Pepper to taste**
**4 cups milk**
**8-10 slices bacon, cooked and crumbled**
**1 teaspoon dry mustard**
**½ cup mushrooms, sliced**
**½ cup tomatoes, chopped and peeled**

*Preparation:*

1. Preheat oven to 325°F.

2. Butter 9 x 13-inch baking dish.

3. Arrange bread in dish and sprinkle with cheese.

4. Beat together eggs, milk, mustard, salt and onion powder with pepper to taste and pour evenly over the bread and cheese.

5. Sprinkle with bacon, mushrooms and tomatoes.

6. Cover and chill up to 24 hours (less chilling time is okay).

7. Bake, uncovered, until set; about 1 hour. Cover with foil tent if it begins to over-brown.

*Enjoy!*

## About the Contributor...

Mary Ellen McNish is the general secretary of the American Friends Service Committee, founded in 1917 by Quakers to "provide conscientious objectors with an opportunity to aid civilian war victims...." With humor, grace and calm balance, Mary Ellen oversees the AFSC's programs and projects in more than 22 countries and 46 cities in the United States. She's also a terrific public speaker and clear and concise writer who makes difficult issues easy to follow. The AFSC is committed to the principles of non-violence and justice, and for its work received the Nobel Peace Prize in 1947. For more on the AFSC, please go to: www.afsc.org.

# RIGOBERTA MENCHÚ TUM

*"Chilim is a recipe from Mayan kitchens in Guatemala."*

## Chilim
## (Pork Ribs with Tomatoes and Chile)
*(Serves six)*

*Ingredients:*

**2 pounds pork ribs**
**6 medium tomatoes**
**4 tomatillos**
**3 large chilies, seeded**
**1 dark red chili**
**1 large onion, chopped**
**1½ cups water (to cook ribs)**
**2 cups water (to cook tomatoes)**

*Preparation:*

1. Cut ribs into small portions. In a large skillet, bring 1½ cups of water to a boil. Add ribs to water; cook until the water is absorbed. Turn to low heat and continue cooking ribs in their grease.

2. Add chopped onion to sauté as ribs continue cooking. If there is excess grease when ribs are cooked, discard it.

3. Cook the tomatoes and tomatillos in two cups of water. Once cooked, chop them up in the same water in which they have been cooked.

4. Remove seeds from chilies and sauté them in a separate skillet. Once cooked, chop them up and add them to the tomatoes. The chilies are to give flavor and a touch of heat, so add accordingly.

5. Add the tomato/chili sauce to the pan with the ribs; cook together another five minutes or just until the sauce begins to boil.

*Serve and enjoy!*

## About the Contributor...

Rigoberta Menchú Tum is an indigenous Guatemalan human rights and peace activist who received the Nobel Peace Prize in 1992 for her work for social justice for her people and for working to bring peace to Guatemala after years of civil war. Rigoberta lost many members of her family during the war including both her parents, two brothers and a sister-in-law. After receipt of the Peace Prize, she created the Menchú Tum Foundation to promote the rights of indigenous people and continue the search for real peace. Although a fierce defender of the rights of her people, she is quick to smile and has an infectious laugh. In 2007, Rigoberta Menchú Tum ran for President of Guatemala, the first Mayan woman to do so, campaigning around the country for the rights of all Guatemalans. She is the author of several books including *I, Rigoberta Menchú* – if you haven't read it, you should. Rigoberta is also one of the founders of the Nobel Women's Initiative with sister Nobel Peace Laureates Jody Williams, Shirin Ebadi, Wangari Maathai, Betty Williams, and Mairead Maguire in January 2006. For more information about her, please go to: www.frmt.org or www.nobelwomensinitiative.org.

# PAT MITCHELL

"*Peace is more than the opposite of war and more than the absence of conflict or violence. Peace, like power, is best felt within first and then moved outward with actions that invite collaboration, consultation, negotiation. Peace doesn't just happen. Peace has to be made and it sometimes means letting go or stepping aside, but in order to be long lasting, it has to also mean standing up for a just and equitable peace. Any other kind will fail.*

*Since I haven't cooked since 1970 or so, it was hard to find one of my recipes, but I did find my favorite from my Grandmother and my mom, too. It is the cake they baked for every special event and I've even done it myself a couple of times. It's a Southern tradition…hard as hell to make, but worth it.*"

## Grandmother's Red Velvet Cake

*Ingredients:*

Cake:
- 1 teaspoon vanilla
- 1 cup buttermilk
- 1 teaspoon salt
- 2½ cups cake flour
- ½ pound (2 sticks) butter
- 4 tablespoons red food coloring
- 2 tablespoons cocoa
- 2 cups sugar
- 2 eggs
- ½ teaspoon baking soda
- 1 tablespoon vinegar

Icing:
- 2 cups confectioner's sugar
- 1 stick butter, softened
- 1 cup melted marshmallows
- 1 cup shredded coconut
- 1 cup chopped pecans
- 1 cup cream cheese

## Preparation:

*Cake:*

1. Preheat oven to 350°F.
2. Beat eggs; add sugar.
3. Mix cocoa and food coloring.
4. Add butter and egg mixture, mix well.
5. Sift together flour and salt. Add to creamed mixture alternately with buttermilk.
6. Blend in vanilla.
7. In a small bowl, combine soda and vinegar and add to mixture.
8. Pour into three 8-inch round greased and floured pans.
9. Bake for 20 to 25 minutes, until toothpick comes out clean.

*Icing:*

1. Blend cream cheese and butter.
2. Add marshmallows and sugar; blend.
3. Fold in coconut and nuts.
4. Spread between layers and on top and sides of cooled cake.

## About the Contributor...

Pat Mitchell currently is the President and Chief Executive Officer of The Paley Center for Media, which leads the discussion about the cultural, creative, and social significance of television, radio, and emerging platforms for the professional community and media-interested public. She brought to that position a wealth of experience as a correspondent and in broadcasting; she was the first woman CEO of PBS, the Public Broadcasting System. Pat strongly supports the empowerment of women and is a committed advocate for positive social change. She has a gorgeous smile, a fantastic mind and is an awesome interviewer and moderator – talents she has generously used as a close friend of the Nobel Women's Initiative and V-Day, among many other organizations working to empower women. To list her achievements and recognitions would take volumes, so we will simply note that in 2008, she was inducted into the Broadcast and Cable Hall of Fame. For more information about Pat Mitchell and her work, please go to: www.paleycenter.org

# PRINCESS DINA &
# PRINCE MIRED RA'AD AL-HUSSEIN

## Mujadara
## (Rice, Lentils & Onions)

*Ingredients:*

**3 pounds white onions, sliced moderately thin**
**2 tablespoons butter**
**2 tablespoons vegetable oil**
**1½ cups brown or green lentils (not red lentils)**
**2 cups long grain white or brown rice**
**1¼ tablespoons ground cinnamon**
**¼ tablespoon ground cumin**
**Salt and pepper to taste**
**Flat leaf parsley for serving**

*Preparation:*

1.  Melt the butter along with the oil and 1 teaspoon of salt in largest available skillet and add the onions.  Set heat on medium-low and stir occasionally until very soft, about 20 minutes.  Turn heat to medium high and keep cooking and stirring often until deeply browned, another 20 minutes or more.

2. Meanwhile, cook the rice and the lentils separately according to your usual method. The lentils need to be watched carefully. You don't want them still crunchy, but you definitely want to retain their shape. Some people cook the rice and lentils together but this won't give you enough control over the texture.

3. When everything is cooked, fold the rice, lentils, spices, half of the onions and more salt and pepper together in a large bowl. Taste and adjust seasonings.

4. To serve, form a large mound, top with the remaining onions and chopped parsley, a twist of pepper, and a few grains of sea salt.  Pass a bowl of yogurt to mix in as desired.  It's really good at room temperature, and just gets better after a day in the refrigerator!

## About the Contributors...

Prince Mired Ra'ad Al-Hussein is the Chairman of Jordan's National Center for Demining and Rehabilitation (NCDR), which is the national demining authority for the country. The Prince also served as the President of the 8th Meeting of States Parties to the Mine Ban Treaty, which was held in Jordan in November of 2007. The annual meetings are important events where governments and civil society come together to assess the progress and remaining challenges to achieving a world free of the threat of landmines. Princess Dina joined the Al-Hussein Society for the Habilitation/ Rehabilitation of the Physically Challenged, which seeks to utilize the skills of physically challenged women. In 2003, the Princess became Director of the King Hussein Cancer Foundation (KHCF). They are the warm, loving and generous parents of three children. For information about the NCDR, please go to: www.ncdr.org.jo. And for the KHCF, go to: www.khcc.jo/The_King_Hussein_Cancer_Foundation1.aspx.

# PRESIDENT JOSÉ RAMOS-HORTA

*"This is eaten at least once a week in East Timor. It is a food recommended for only children above the age of one!"*

## Timorese Fish Balls

*Ingredients:*

**10.5 ounces (about 1½ cups) of CSB (A corn-soya blend distributed by World Food Program)**
**Vegetable oil**
**About 2 cups of water**
**1 tablespoon salt**
**½ tablespoon pepper**
**1 medium size fish fillet**

*Preparation:*

1. Mix CSB with salt and pepper, then add water.
2. Add the fish fillet to the mixture.
3. With two soup spoons, make small fish balls from the mixture.
4. Fry the fish balls in the vegetable oil.
5. Once the balls are fried, place them on a paper towel to soak up any excess oil.

*The fish balls are best served warm!*

## About the Contributor...

José Ramos-Horta is the second President of Timor-Leste (East Timor) and took office in May of 2007; prior to that he served as Prime Minister. In 1996 he received the Nobel Peace Prize for his decades of work from exile to resolve the conflict that had been going on as his country sought independence from Indonesia. As President, he has sought to bring sustainable peace and stability to his small country – no small task given the poverty in the country after so many years of oppression. Jose Ramos Horta survived an attempt on his life in February 2008 in which he was seriously wounded. Despite his responsibilities as president of his country, Jose maintains his wry sense of humor and continues to work actively with PeaceJam to help inspire youth to work for a better world. For more information about the President and Timor-Leste, please go to: www.timor-leste.gov.ti/. For an interesting interview with President Ramos Horta, check out: www.youtube.com/watch?v=JT3X6IRjk9A. You'll also find more about the President at: www.peacejam.org.

# JUDY
## RAND

*"Sharing a good recipe is spreading good will. Good stories and fond memories come with these recipes. I hope they will do the same over time for you."*

## Chicken Dijon with Capers

*Ingredients:*

**6 small chicken thighs, boneless and skinless**
**About ½ cup chicken stock**
**⅓ cup white wine**
**1 tablespoon (or more) Dijon mustard**
**Capers (I mash them up a little with a fork)**

*Preparation:*

1. Trim off as much fat as possible from the chicken thighs (scissors work great!). What you can't trim off becomes part of the sauce.

2. Brown them slightly on both sides in a hot frying pan; just a couple of minutes per side.

3. Pour in chicken stock; let simmer for 8-10 minutes – turn chicken once during that time. Remove chicken. Most of the stock should be boiled away.

4. Deglaze the pan with white wine.

5. Turn heat to low or off. Stir in Dijon mustard. Add capers. You can put the chicken back in and heat everything together.

*The sauce ends up being more like a yummy brown gooey coating.*

## Mango-Avocado Salsa

*Ingredients:*

**Equal parts mango and avocado, cut into chunks**
**¼ to ⅓ cup chopped fresh cilantro**
**1 tablespoon olive oil**
**Coarse salt to taste**

## Preparation:

1. Gently stir all ingredients together.
   *Makes a terrific accompaniment to fish. Enjoy.*

## About the Contributor...

Judy Rand is a fantastic professional photographer who just happens to be photographer for much of the work of the Nobel Women's Initiative. She shoots in the studio and on location and no matter where she is, she does it beautifully. She has shot, for example, the 2005 US Open Snowboarding Championship in Stratton, Vermont, and a three-week delegation of the Nobel Women's Initiative on the Thai/Burma border, in Ethiopia, South Sudan and the Darfur refugee camps in Chad in July-August of 2008. Judy is kind and generous and a fantastic friend; she has made me lol (laugh out loud for those not in the know) for years and years and years. Please go to her website, www. jrandimagesinc.com to see some of her work. You'll also find Judy Rand photos at: www.nobelwomensinitiative.org.

# MARKUS REITERER

*"Peace ends where violence begins. And violence almost always starts in language: We fight against corruption. We wage a war against drugs. We strike against crime. We engage in battle against climate change. We even fight poverty and hunger (not yet – at least – the poor and hungry!).*

*We aggressively pursue our aims. We combat whatever financial crisis. We attack a problem head-on. We lead a battle for customers and clients. We enter a fight against HIV/AIDS and malaria.*

*Yes, if this is how peace ends, how does it begin? Perhaps as soon as we start to comprehend that language is not just another martial art. Why don't we start to address climate change, to act with determination and vigor against a financial crisis and prevent and alleviate poverty and hunger? Words, you might say, just words. And, yes, I agree. But they are words of peace, not war. And that's a start.*

*I propose a recipe for bread. It's a bread of fusion, a mix of different tastes, ideas and cultures starting from central Europe and working its way through the Mediterranean to the Middle East by adding herbs and spices, sun-dried tomatoes, olives and feta cheese."*

## Mediterranean Bread Roll

*Ingredients:*

*Dough:*

- 3½ cups flour (whole grain if available)
- 1 cup of warm water
- 1 package of dry yeast
- 4 tablespoons olive oil
- 1 teaspoon salt
- 1 teaspoon ground coriander

*Filling:*

- Handful of sun-dried tomatoes
- Handful of olives
- ¾ cup feta cheese
- Oregano
- Sesame seeds (optional)
- Thyme (if you can get wild thyme – all the better!)
- Rosemary
- Ground black pepper
- Cumin seeds

## Preparation:

*Dough:*

1. Preheat oven to 350°F.
2. Dissolve the yeast in the water and let it rise for 15 minutes.
3. Add the remaining ingredients for the dough and knead it for at least five minutes.
4. Put the bowl with the dough in a warm spot; cover it with a damp cloth, and let it rise for about one hour.
5. Knead the dough again and put it on a lightly floured surface.
6. Roll out the dough (use a rolling pin or an empty bottle of wine) until it is fairly thin (less than half an inch).

*Filling:*

7. Splash some olive oil on the dough.
8. Spread the diced sun-dried tomatoes over the dough.
9. Cut the olives into small pieces and add them.
10. Do the same with the crumbled feta. By now your bread looks a bit like a pizza.
11. Add the herbs.
12. Form a roll (so your bread looks like a wrap), brush on olive oil and bake it for 30 to 40 minutes.

*Enjoy!*

## About the Contributor...

Markus Reiterer is an Austrian diplomat who is currently stationed as his country's Embassy in Washington, DC. Before coming to Washington, Markus represented his government in the ongoing efforts to rid the world of landmines at various meetings related to the Mine Ban Treaty, and where he has really left his mark is his work on victim assistance, particularly in the development and negotiation of the 2008 Convention on Cluster Munitions. The sections of that treaty that deal with assistance to survivors of the weapon are groundbreaking and a significant advance over similar sections in the Mine Ban Treaty. Markus Reiterer played a critical role in making that happen. Markus has a great sense of humor and when he's not busy being a diplomat, he is a fantastic cook and he also can play a mean piano! With more diplomats like Markus Reiterer, the world would be a much better place. To find out more about the Convention on Cluster Munitions, please go to the Cluster Munition Coalition's website at: www.stopclustermunitions.org.

# JOHN RODSTED

*"Being hungry turns you into a rumbling void. Exhaustion rolls on with the hunger 'til every action churns a thumping nausea. Dreams are of food but if it comes it can't be eaten. Stomachs contract 'til there's only pain and only space for memories.*

*Cambodians know hunger; they know the gnawing in the pits of their bowels. They also know the pain of dysentery from so much water but all of it foul. You get sicker and sicker, weaker and weaker, always dreaming of a better world, a better life, any life but the one you are in. You'll soon die. We all die, it's just you will do it sooner than others. This might be a release from the pain, but that's only a thought held by those who have never held onto life by the edges of fingernails. No one wants to die.*

*War complicates hunger. If you could grow food, then someone makes sure you can't. Peace becomes the partner of food. If there is peace you can eat. When peace came, you found mutilation as war left landmines, the ultimate perversion to safety and a future. 'Enough is enough! Madness must stop.' With peace comes food, with food safety, with safety a future.*

*I used walk in hunger and live in war, always fearing landmines, but my dreams were of food and warmth. Whenever I re-entered the world, I would cook for my friends. Cooking should never be rushed, as it's a ritual to be shared with love."*

## The Brew is the Bog & the Bog is a Brew, from John to You

*Ingredients:*

> Bottle of red wine
> 1 large brown onion, diced
> 1 green capsicum (bell pepper), diced
> 1-2 garlic cloves
> Olive oil
> 1 pound ground beef
> Large fistful of mushrooms, diced
> Fine ground pepper (white or black makes no difference – but be generous; two teaspoons will give scent)
> 1 cup of water (at least)
> 14 ounces (just under 2 cups) thick tomato paste
> 1 heaping tablespoon of dried thyme
> 1 heaping tablespoon of oregano
> Dried minced chili to taste (not a "pinch" is needed, but a generous amount for warmth – at least a teaspoon)
> 2 beef stock cubes (to give body to the mix)

## Pasta
## Fresh parmesan

*Preparation:*

1. Pour yourself a glass of wine, a large one.

2. Sauté onion, green capsicum, and garlic in olive oil until it's tender and clear.

3. Add ground beef; all's turned till they are one.

4. Roll mushrooms through the mixture to earthen the flavor. Stir and brown.

5. Add ground pepper. Stir.

6. Pour another large glass of wine, this one's for the brew. At least one third of the bottle will be needed for its heart. Now the same goes for water, at least a cup in. The whole brew is mixing and you are past the beginning.

7. Turn up the heat until it is simmering, then, turn it down (oh so low) again.

8. Add the tomato paste; it will turn it to rouge, then in goes the dried thyme. Thyme needs its friend oregano, so match the dose.

9. We are lacking fire, so chili is added to taste. Last but not least, add beef stock cubes.

10. Now the magic ingredient time; it's a brew. Cover, with a wooden spoon holding the lid ajar, and simmer for at least one and half hours till the whole mix reduces to a brew. After all – it is a brew. If it reduces too fast then add more wine, or water, and continue till the right time comes, one hour and a half, or ninety minutes, or five thousand four hundred seconds – whichever comes first.

11. Now sit and talk to your family and friends till it's done. Give them some wine too. You can take turns in stirring and becoming peaceful.

*Serve over al dente pasta with fresh parmesan on top. It's even better the next day. Oh did I forget, look someone in the eyes and tell them something special. Bon appetite!*

## About the Contributor...

John Rodsted.....John Rodsted.....Where to start? Where to end? John is almost indescribably unique. He's from Australia, but we try not to hold that against him. He's an outstanding campaigner against landmines, cluster bombs – just about anything evil and rotten. He's also a terrific photographer and has been chronicling landmines and cluster bombs, their survivors, and committed campaign activists since forever it seems. John, along with his "significant other" Mette Eliseussen, who is also a contributor to this cookbook, embarked on a journey across the United States in the "Ban Bus" in 1997 to build support for the Mine Ban Treaty. Eleven years later they did it again, this time across Europe in support of the 2008 Cluster Munition Convention that bans cluster bombs. You can see them and read John's "two minute history" of the ban bus at: http://thebanbus.org/the-ban-bus/. You can find some of John's photography in the image gallery of the International Campaign to Ban Landmines at: www.icbl.org.

# JULIANNA ROOSEVELT

*"This is the original recipe from Grandmère and it always tasted so very good. Though I make this with lady fingers and add some vanilla to the cream before I whip it, Grandmère was making sure stale bread did not go to waste! The berries for this recipe were usually picked in the wild, tart and fresh, or shipped from Campobello Island, New Brunswick."*

## Blueberry (Huckleberry) Pudding
## By Mrs. Eleanor Roosevelt
## As remembered by
## her great granddaughter
## Julianna Roosevelt

### Ingredients:

**Day old bread**
**Berries, sweetened, stewed**
**Whipped cream/heavy cream**

### Preparation:

1. In a bake pan or casserole, place a layer of bread (remove the crust if you like), then a layer of sweetened, stewed berries, and keep alternating bread and berries until you have the desired thickness with a layer of berries on the top.

2. Chill overnight or longer if desired. Serve with whipped cream or heavy cream.

*Fresh berries from your own garden or the farmer's market are perfect; in fact the mushed, over-ripe ones are best.*

*(Note: This recipe also appears in the Val-Kill Cookbook.)*

## About the Contributor...

Julianna Roosevelt helps people create organic kitchen gardens through her business "An Edible Garden" in Los Angeles, California. "An Edible Garden" is the culmination of years of relationships with gardens, which has evolved from avocation to vocation. Her work "responds to both her political and philosophical beliefs that now more than ever we need to be able to feed ourselves and our families in healthy and creative ways." Given Julianna's family history, it is no surprise that she feels a strong sense of social responsibility. Before her work with gardens and food, she was an educational therapist who worked with children with learning disabilities. For more information about Julianna and her "Edible Garden," please go to: www.anediblegarden.com.

# DR. SIMA SAMAR

## Qabuli Palau
## (Chicken with Basmati Rice & Carrots)
*(Serves eight)*

*Ingredients:*

    **2 cups Basmati rice**
    **6 cups water, for rice**
    **¼ cup ghee or butter**
    **1 yellow onion, sliced thinly**
    **3 pounds chicken pieces, skinless**
    **2 tablespoons tomato paste**
    **2½ teaspoons salt**
    **1 teaspoon garlic, crushed**
    **3½ cups water**
    **1 tablespoon garam masala**
*Garnish:*
    **2 carrots, shredded or julienned into matchsticks**
    **½ cup raisins**
    **⅓ cup slivered almonds**
    **½ cup hot water**

*Preparation:*

1. Pre-cook rice: Rinse Basmati rice several times in cold water until water is clear.

2. Bring 6 cups of water to a boil and add Basmati. Cook for only 6 minutes. Drain rice and set aside.

3. In a large skillet, heat ghee or butter. Add onion slices and caramelize, cooking until dark brown. This will take awhile.

4. Remove onions and set aside, leaving most of the ghee or butter in the pan.

5. Add chicken pieces to skillet and brown on all sides. Remove chicken, saving ghee.

6. Place chicken pieces in a good-sized pot, adding salt, garlic and 3½ cups water to the chicken. Bring to a boil, cover, and simmer over medium heat for 20-30 minutes or until chicken is tender. Remove chicken and set aside in a warm place. Reserve chicken liquid.

7.  While chicken is cooking on the stove, in a food processor, blend caramelized onion with ½ cups water or chicken liquid, tomato paste and salt.  Pour tomato paste mixture back into chicken broth and boil for 10 minutes.  Add rice and garam masala to chicken broth mixture. Cover and simmer rice until liquid is reduced and rice is tender.

8.  While the rice is simmering, cook shredded carrot in the skillet with left over ghee until golden brown.  Drain ghee from skillet, add raisins, almonds, and ½ cup of water to the carrots and cook until all the water is reduced.

9.  Place rice on a platter or in a large, shallow bowl.  Arrange chicken pieces on top of the rice and garnish with the carrot-raisin-almond mixture.

*Serve and enjoy.*

## About the Contributor...

Dr. Sima Samar, a medical doctor, chairs the Afghan Independent Human Rights Commission and has served as the UN Special Rapporteur on the situation of human rights in Sudan since 2005.  After fleeing with her child to Pakistan in 1984, where she lived in exile, Sima returned to Afghanistan in 2002 and was Deputy President and Minister for Women's Affairs in the interim government led by Hamid Karzai.  Because she is a forceful advocate for women's rights and education, she did not last long in the government. She founded the Shuhada Organization in 1989; it has six clinics and three hospitals in Afghanistan all decided to the health care of women and girls. We first worked together on a UN High Level Mission on Darfur for the Human Rights Council in early 2007.  Her humor, intelligence and wealth of experience on the situation in the Sudan made her an invaluable member of the team on what proved to be a very difficult mission.  Sima also was a member of the Nobel Women's Initiative's delegation to the Thai/Burma border in 2008. When she received the John F. Kennedy Profile in Courage Award in 2004, she began her acceptance speech with these words:  "A journalist this winter asked me what do I consider to be my biggest success - of what achievement am I most proud?  My answer is that my greatest success is that I am still alive, that I am still in Afghanistan and that I am still imposing myself on the men in power."  You'll find her entire speech at: www.jfklibrary.org/Education+and+Public+Programs/Profile+in+Courage+Award.  For more information about Dr. Sima Samar and the Shuhada Organization, please go to: www.shuhada.org.af/Content.asp?id=dr.Sima.

# NORA SHEETS and her Fourth Grade "Proud Students Against Landmines"

*"The landmine kids have been awesome....they are so with it....When I had a meeting for students interested in joining for the new school year, 27 kids showed up (we already had 30!). We will be working with Alison and Jose/Landmines Blow! to raise funds for our third water well in Cambodia in October and the kids are working on the cluster munitions awareness campaign. March 2009 marked our 10th year of Students Against Landmines at St. Francis.....Here are some offerings for the 'Peace' cookbook! Hope they help! We had fun thinking of ideas and takes on the word 'peace.'"*

*"Peace is when everyone loves and cares for each other."* Gretchen, 4th grade, age 10

*"Peace means to me harmony and an end to all violence."* Erin, 4th grade, age 10

*"Peace to me means ending the war. It means having a treaty to end fighting. It also means to be aware of dangerous actions among countries."* Makenna, 4th grade, age 10

*"Peace happens when you take care of others in need."* Paige, 4th grade, age 10

*"Peace means that if you go to another place, you won't get hurt just because they don't know you."* Logan, 4th grade, age 10

*"Peace is not just about talking but about taking action."* Vinitha, 4th grade, age 10

*"Peace means freedom in today's society. I feel it is also being peaceful of mind and spirit."* Nina, age 12

*"A peaceful world is one of diversity and equality."* Jessica, age 13

*"Peace means being able to be yourself. It also means sharing what you have with others."* Vanessa, age 13

# Beets, Love and Understanding
## (Beet Chips)

*Ingredients:*

**4 beets**
**1 tablespoon olive oil**
**Salt to taste**

*Preparation:*

1. Preheat oven to 400°F.
2. Clean beets (do not peel them). Slice thinly.
3. Toss with olive oil and salt.
4. Spread evenly on a cookie sheet.
5. Roast 45 to 60 minutes, turning halfway through, until crisp.
   *Note: You can add different seasonings and spices!*

# Whirled Peas
## (Split Pea Soup)

*Ingredients:*

**⅓ cup chopped celery**
**⅓ cup chopped onions**
**⅓ cup chopped carrots**
**2 cups dried split peas**
**1 tablespoon olive oil**
**¼ teaspoon thyme**
**1½ quarts vegetable stock**
**Salt and pepper to taste**

*Preparation:*

1. Sauté the carrot, celery, onion and thyme in the olive oil.
2. Add the split peas and vegetable stock. Bring the ingredients to a boil.
3. Simmer until the peas are tender (it may take up to an hour).
4. Put ⅔ of the soup in a blender and blend until it is puréed.
5. Add in the remaining ⅓ mixture. Return to stove and heat on medium high until thickened.
6. Add salt and additional pepper to taste.

# "Paz" the Cookies

## Ingredients:

- **1 cup butter**
- **2½ cups flour**
- **½ cup powdered sugar**
- **1 cup nuts, finely chopped (walnuts or pecans)**
- **1 teaspoon vanilla**
- **¼ teaspoon almond extract**

## Preparation:

1. Preheat oven to 350°F.
2. Cream butter, sugar, vanilla and almond extract.
3. Add flour, salt and nuts.
4. Roll dough into balls.
5. Bake 12-15 minutes.
6. Remove from oven and top with powdered sugar.

# Let There be Pesto
# (Pesto Spaghetti Squash)

## Ingredients:

- **Leaves from 2 bunches of fresh basil**
- **2 tablespoons pine nuts**
- **1 garlic clove**
- **½ cup extra-virgin olive oil**
- **½ cup freshly grated parmesan cheese**
- **Salt and freshly ground black pepper**
- **Spaghetti squash**
- **Shredded parmesan cheese, for garnish**

## Preparation:

1. Combine the basil, pine nuts, garlic and olive oil in a blender and blend. Add the cheese, salt and pepper and blend again.
2. Place ½ spaghetti squash in microwave for 7-8 minutes. Repeat with the other half. Remove seeds and stringy portion. Use fork to pull squash off in strands. Place in large serving bowl. Add the pesto and toss.
3. Top with shredded parmesan cheese.

# Give Peas a Chance
## (Old Fashioned Creamed Peas)

*Ingredients:*

**2 boxes of frozen peas – do NOT thaw (If possible, use 2
pounds shelled fresh peas)
2 cups of heavy cream
1 teaspoon of sugar
1½ tablespoons of flour
⅓ cup evaporated milk
1 stick of butter
Salt and pepper**

*Preparation:*

1. Put frozen peas in a large saucepan.

2. Add 2 cups of heavy cream. Bring to a simmer. Add a teaspoon of sugar. Cover and simmer for 10 minutes.

3. In a small bowl, mix 1½ tablespoons of flour with ⅓ cup evaporated milk until smooth.

4. Remove peas from heat and add flour mixture.

5. Return to heat and cook on low until flour mixture is thoroughly cooked and peas are thickened (about 10 minutes).

6. Add one stick of butter and stir to blend. Add black pepper and salt to taste.

*About the Contributors...*

Where to begin! If all teachers were like Nora Sheets, we would indeed live in a peaceful world. Nora is an art teacher at the St. Francis Catholic School in Morgantown, West Virginia where she has been working with her students to ban landmines and cluster bombs for a decade. With her passion, compassion and hilarious sense of humor and love of life, it's no surprise that her students wanted to take up the issue of landmines and form a group of "Proud Students Against Landmines." Now they do even more and raise support for well-building activities, partnering with Alison Bock and Jose de Arteaga (also recipe contributors) of Landmines Blow! It's people like Nora Sheets and her students who keep me inspired to continue my own work as an activist. For a article on Nora and her "kids" check out: www.hdic.jmu.edu/JOURNAL/12.2/mip/shane/shane.htm; also for more information on Nora, please go to: http://falcon.sfcc.pvt.k12.wv.us/faculty/nsheets.shtm. Also, you can check out: www.landminesblow.com.

# EMILY SIMON

*"In these times of perceived financial instability in the United States, we need to remember that most people on this planet confront economic instability day in and day out, month after month and year after year. Lack of ability to acquire basic needs, including food and water, is oppression of the worst kind and will prevent a lasting peace. When we talk about a basic redistribution of excess wealth, we have to remember that it will make a nicer place for us all to live."*

## Salmon Curry

*Ingredients:*

**Oil**
**Garlic, sliced**
**2 teaspoons cumin seeds**
**10-12 curry leaves, if not available 6 bay leaves**
**1 teaspoon black mustard seeds**
**1 teaspoon coriander**
**2 pounds salmon filet, skinless and cut into cubes**
**2 tablespoons tomato paste**
**½ teaspoon sugar**
**1 teaspoon garam masala (if you don't have that, put in a bit more of coriander, cumin, turmeric)**
**A bunch of coriander leaves, chopped**
**Chilies to taste**
**1 teaspoon tamarind paste – hard to find but worth it**
**1 can of coconut milk**

*Preparation:*

1. Put oil, garlic, cumin, mustard seeds, and coriander in a frying pan or wok. Fry until you smell the flavor. Do not burn.

2. Add curry leaves and salmon to pan and fry for 5 minutes.

3. Mix tomato paste, sugar, garam masala, coriander leaves, chilies, tamarind paste, and coconut milk in a bowl. Pour into salmon.

4. Cook until salmon is cooked through. This should be about another 3-4 minutes. *Serve with...*

# The Best Rice You Will Ever Eat

*Ingredients:*

**2 cups Basmati or long grain rice, rinsed and drained**
**1 package of frozen spinach, chopped small**
**1 bouillon cube**
**1 can coconut milk**
**1 cup water**

*Preparation:*

1. Put all together in a pot; cover with a lid; bring to a boil. Stir. Simmer for about 15 minutes. Turn off burner.

2. Let rest. *Fluff and eat!*

*About the Contributor...*

Emily Simon is a long-time activist and generous philanthropist. She has supported environmental and political causes including TreePeople, a non-profit organization which was the first to actually understand and put into action the idea of a sustainable ecosystem supported by trees and watershed. In fact, we first met at a Tree People event in LA and became almost immediately fast friends. She now is focused on bringing together community through theater. Emily is frighteningly smart, funny as hell and knows her way around a kitchen as well as anyone I know – well, actually, better than most. Having the opportunity to share an Emily Simon-made meal isn't something that should be passed up lightly. Emily is also a supporter of the Nobel Women's Initiative. In her other life, Emily is an attorney and when she practiced represented some pretty "hot" bands and musicians.

# AMBASSADOR
# SATNAM SINGH

## Chicken Marsala Delhi Style
*(Serves six)*

*Ingredients:*

**2 pounds of chicken, preferably boneless, cut into small pieces**
**2 medium sized onions, chopped**
**1 medium sized tomato, made into purée**
**2 teaspoons garlic paste**
**2 teaspoons ginger paste**
**10-12 whole cashew nuts, roasted**
**2 tablespoons cashew nuts, ground**
**10-12 whole almonds, roasted**
**2 tablespoons almonds, ground**
**1 cup plain yogurt (can be omitted for kosher meal)**
**4-5 tablespoons cooking oil**
**1 teaspoon garam masala (recipe below)**
**1 teaspoon coriander powder**
**½ teaspoon chili powder**
**Salt to taste**

*Preparation:*

1. Heat the oil; add chopped onions and cook until golden brown. Add a cup of water and cook until almost dry.

2. Add ginger, garlic, turmeric, cumin seed, coriander powder, chili powder. Stir for about one minute. Add ground cashews and almonds, making sure it does not stick.

3. Add chicken pieces; salt to taste, mix thoroughly.

4. Cook for 10-15 minutes, adding some water to avoid sticking.

5. Add tomato purée; cook for another 5-7 minutes.

6. Add beaten yogurt (paste); cook until it is done.

7. Garnish with cashew nuts, almonds, and green coriander.

*Serve hot with rice or chapatti (Indian bread).*

# Garam Masala

*Ingredients:*
- **10-12 peppercorns**
- **4-5 brown cardamoms**
- **4-5 cloves**
- **1 cinnamon stick**

*Preparation:*
1. Grind ingredients together in an electric grinder.
   *(Editors' note: store left-over spice in spice jar.)*

*About the Contributor...*

Retired Indian Ambassador Satnam Singh has served as diplomatic advisor to the International Campaign to Ban Landmines (ICBL) since early 2004 when he expressed his interest in helping the ICBL reach out to countries that had not yet joined the Mine Ban Treaty. Satnam brings a wealth of experience to his work with the ICBL, having held senior diplomatic posts in countries around the world. His commitment to ridding the world of the horror of antipersonnel landmines also comes from his personal experience with the weapon, having lost a leg to a landmine while serving in the Indian military. His first hand experience as a landmine survivor coupled with his skills as a diplomat have made Ambassador Satnam Singh an invaluable part of the ICBL. For more information on the work of the ICBL, please go to: www.icbl.org. To read about his work on a July 2009 trip to Mongolia and see a photograph of the distinguished Ambassador in his usual sartorial splendor, go to: www.icbl.org/index.php/icbl/Library/News-Articles/Universal/mongolia.

# SUSANNAH SIRKIN

"The 'refugee diet' for Darfuri women who struggle to survive in camps on the Chad side of Sudan's border consists of 2,100 kilocalories of sorghum, salt, sugar and oil. Six years and counting, this is what they are given to eat, day in and day out. By the time they trade some of their rations to grind the grain and add some milk or a bit of meat for their children, or sell some for other supplies, the caloric level is so meager that they are constantly hungry. Women interviewed by my colleagues from Physicians for Human Rights hid in their clothing the few biscuits offered during the sessions so that they could bring them back to their children.

Yet, these women were proud, dignified and self-sufficient farmers in their native villages in Darfur. They farmed, harvested and rode on donkeys to nearby markets to sell their crops and buy fruits and vegetables produced in the lush Jebel Marra region of Darfur, for instance. During a visit to Darfur's capital in 2006, a doctor presented me with a basketful of the most delicious oranges I have ever tasted – a product of his home village there.

The refugee diet adds to the profound depression experienced by Darfuri women who remember the nightmare of the burning of their villages, the forced flight from their homes, and the trauma of sexual violence. In the camps, they still live in fear of ongoing violence and stigma. They yearn for home, and they long for the pleasure of planting, harvesting, cooking and communal eating.

My fantasy recipe for these women comes from a favorite poem by the Chilean poet, Pablo Neruda, 'The Great Tablecloth' (El Gran Mantel),

'Let us sit down to eat
With all those who haven't eaten;
Let us spread great tablecloths,
Put salt in the lakes of the world,
Set up planetary bakeries,
Tables with strawberries in snow,
And a plate like the moon itself
From which we can all eat.
For now I ask nothing more
Than the justice of eating.'"

# Fantasy Recipe for the Women of Darfur
## (Mesas Con Frescas en la Nieve – Tables with Strawberries in Snow)

*Ingredients:*
**Strawberries**
**Whipped cream**
**Sugar**

### *The Darfur Version:*
## Ambrosia
## (The food of the gods that humans deserve)

*Ingredients:*
**6 Jebel Marra (or other) oranges**
**1 cup of coconut, shredded.**

*Preparation:*
1. Slice oranges and combine with coconut.
  *Chill and serve.*

*About the Contributor...*

Susannah Sirkin is the Deputy Director of Physicians for Human Rights (PHR), a position she has held since she joined PHR in 1987, shortly after the non-profit organization was formed. Susannah is absolutely tireless in her dedication and commitment to defending and promoting human rights around the world. She brings much experience, wit and wisdom to any project she is involved in. She has organized and carried out investigations of human rights violations in countries around the world – including her recent work documenting crimes against humanity and the systematic and widespread use of rape as a tactic in the war in Darfur. Susannah has also documented sexual violence in Bosnia, Sierra Leone, and Thailand. She is a prolific writer and compelling speaker. Susannah Sirkin and PHR were among the original founders of the International Campaign to Ban Ladmines. Sometimes she's even a bit too selfless – as when she passed up the opportunity to go to Oslo for the celebration of the ICBL's receipt of the Nobel Peace Prize in 1997! For more information about Susannah Sirkin and Physicians for Human Rights, check out: www.physiciansforhumanrights.org. Also see: www.savedarfur.org.

# CORNELIO SOMMARUGA

## Risotto Alla Luganese

*(Serves four)*

*Ingredients:*

**7 tablespoons of butter**
**½ onion, cut in thin slices**
**¾ cup rice, vialone or Arborio**
**½ cup red wine**
**4-5 cups beef or chicken broth, hot**
**Saffron to taste**
**1 large cup of boletus mushrooms (If they are dried, soak them in water for one hour; drain.)**
**Parmesan cheese to taste**

*Preparation:*

1. In a large pot, heat half of the butter and sauté onions.

2. Add rice and mix well with onions and butter.

3. Add the wine and stir.

4. Add ⅓ of total broth; continue stirring. Once the liquid disappears, add another ⅓ of broth.

5. Add saffron and continue stirring.

6. When the liquid disappears again, add the last ⅓ of hot broth. Add mushrooms (if dried and soaked, do not include water); stir. If more liquid is needed, add some hot water. The risotto is not to be too dry. Total cooking time should be 20 minutes.

7. After cooking, add second half of butter and a very generous portion of grated parmesan cheese.

## About the Contributor...

Dr. Cornelio Sommaruga is a world-reknown Swiss humanitarian, attorney and former diplomat. He served as the President of the International Committee of the Red Cross (ICRC) from 1987-1999 and in that capacity Cornelio moved the usually neutral ICRC not only to call for a ban on antipersonnel landmines but also to campaign actively to reach that goal. Without his vision and leadership, the global movement to ban landmines would have been severely weakened. Cornelio is charming, witty and loquacious and always brings his depth and breadth of experience to any discussion. When he speaks on humanitarian concerns, he carries his listeners with him. Dr. Cornelio Sommaruga served as the president of the Geneva International Center for Humanitarian Demining from 2000-2008; he currently is honorary president of that institution. For more information please go to www.icrc.org and www.gichd.org.

# ARCHBISHOP DESMOND TUTU

*"I am not interested in picking up crumbs of compassion thrown from the table of someone who considers himself my master. I want the full menu of rights."*

*(Editors' Note: While not specifically for the cookbook, the quote seemed to fit the theme.)*

## Tutu Chicken

*Ingredients:*

3 potatoes
3 pounds of chicken, cut in pieces
3 ounces seasoned flour
2 tablespoons vegetable oil
2 onions, chopped
1 green pepper, sliced
2 large tomatoes, skinned and chopped
1 14-ounce can tomato purée
1 tablespoon curry paste
1 teaspoon Tabasco sauce
1 chicken stock cube
2 cups water

*Preparation:*

1. Preheat oven to 300°F.
2. Boil the potatoes for ten minutes until half cooked. Peel and slice.
3. Coat chicken in seasoned flour. Heat oil in frying pan and brown chicken; remove from pan.
4. Add onions and green pepper to the same pan and cook until soft.
5. Add 4-5 tablespoons of the remaining flour to the pan and cook for 1 minute.
6. Add tomato purée, curry paste, Tabasco sauce, stock cube and sufficient water to make a thick sauce.
7. Put the chicken pieces in a large casserole; cover with the sliced potatoes and the sauce.
8. Cover the casserole and bake for 60 minutes. Serve with rice and a salad.

Archbishop Desmond Tutu is a towering figure in the world of human rights, democracy and freedom and a voice of moral authority in the world. Trying to capture his contributions to create a better world in a few short lines is an impossibility so I will stick to a couple of the most well-known points and you can "google" the rest. In any case, what I love best about the "Arch" is his mischievous sense of humor and his unbelievable faith in the goodness of people. Archbishop Tutu played a key role in the struggle against the apartheid government of South Africa and for his work was recognized with the Nobel Peace Prize in 1984. After the transition to democracy, President Nelson Mandela appointed the Archbishop chair of the Truth and Reconciliation Commission which investigated gross violations of human rights under the apartheid government. He is a visiting professor of theology at Emory University in Atlanta, Georgia. When his daughter Naomi heard that he was contributing a recipe, she sent an email telling me to make sure it came from her mother, Leah, because her father cannot cook. You will find a wealth of information about Archbishop Tutu on the internet. Check out the Desmond Tutu Peace Foundation at: www.tutufoundation-usa.org/. To listen to him speak on AIDS, go to: www.youtube.com/watch?v=5bkKg0tp1kg& feature=fvw and on "Reconciling Love," go to: www.youtube.com/watch?v=iV2LURTu3eQ.

# LYNNE TWIST

*"Your request for a recipe came right after my visit to the area of Northern Ecuador where I saw first-hand the destruction to the tropical rainforest and the heartbreaking impact on indigenous people due to the extraction and exploitation of oil. It is the site of the largest environmental law suit in the world against Chevron/Texaco. The devastation is horrific and the people, men, women, and children are all sick with different forms of cancer.*

*It made me realize once again how our dependence on and addiction to oil continues to drive much of the destruction of the environment and the marginalization of peoples everywhere and is at the root of most of the wars raging around the world.*

*People everywhere, indigenous and non-indigenous, just want the space and grace to sit down together with their family and friends and have a good simple meal together. As we all work to end the madness and allow the grace of peace and freedom to show itself, may we break bread together, share hot soup, and nourish one another and appreciate the nourishment of life on earth.*

*As we say in our work with the Pachamama Alliance, may we all bring forth an environmentally sustainable, spiritually fulfilling and socially just human presence on this planet.*

*This is one of those hearty soups that nourishes the body, calms the soul, creates peace in the family and lasts forever."*

## Carrot-Tomato-Lentil-Soup

*Ingredients:*
   **Olive oil**
   **6 large, fresh carrots, shredded**
   **3 large onions, chopped**
   **Fresh rosemary**
   **Fresh thyme**
   **Herbs au Provence**
   **Fresh parsley**
   **Salt and pepper to taste**
   **1½ cups white wine**
   **1 large jar of tomato sauce, (I recommend "Prego" with basil)**
   **8 cups vegetable broth**
   **1½ cups lentils**

## Preparation:

1. Sauté the onions and the shredded carrots in olive oil until soft.

2. Season with fresh rosemary, fresh thyme, salt and pepper, and herbs au Provence.

3. Add white wine and let it simmer for a few minutes.

4. Add tomato sauce and continue to cook.

5. Add the vegetable broth; continue cooking over low heat.

6. Add the lentils and fresh parsley.

7. Simmer over a low heat for an hour and a half or so. Soup is done when lentils are soft.

*Serve with sprinkled parmesan cheese on top. Enjoy!*

## About the Contributor...

Lynne Twist is an activist, author, public speaker – a real woman wonder. With her book, *The Soul of Money*, Lynne has helped people learn how to transform their "relationship with money and life." If you've not read it, in today's economic climate, it is the perfect book to read! But I met Lynne first through PeaceJam and since she has become a key ally and supporter of the work of the Nobel Women's Initiative. Trying to track her down would be a real problem were it not for the internet. If she's not involved in the transformation of the Ecuadorian constitution to recognize the rights of the environment, she's off somewhere with the Pachamama Alliance which works to save tropical rainforests by empowering indigenous people "who are its natural custodians" and to the creation of a "new global vision of equity and sustainability for all." She is genuinely kind, open, warm and giving and her smile lights up a room. To learn more about Lynne Twist and her work, please go to: www.soulofmoney.org; also check out: www.pachamamaalliance.org.

# MARIO VELASQUEZ

*"In Central America, guacamole is made with hard boiled eggs!"*

## Central American Guacamole
### (Serves 8-10)

*Ingredients:*

**8 hard boiled eggs (one egg per avocado)**
**8 avocados**
**1 sweet onion, finely chopped**
**3 limes**
**Salt to taste**

*Preparation:*

1. Mash the hard boiled eggs as finely as possible with a fork in a large mixing bowl.

2. Cut avocados in half; remove the fruit into the mixing bowl. Save the seeds and add them later to ensure the guacamole does not turn brown.

3. Add onion.

4. Squeeze the juice of 3 limes and blend into the creamy green paste until it begins to taste of the lime juice.

5. Add salt and begin to balance the lime taste until your mouth waters.

*It's ready! You can serve with regular chips or lime chips (my favorite) or use the guacamole to compliment any grilled meat.*

## About the Contributor...

Mario Velasquez began working in defense of the people of El Salvador while still a young man in his country. Despite the long line of anti-democratic military officers in his family – his father was a general as was his father before him and his father before him, Mario became a supporter of those struggling for democratic change in his country in the 1970s. After having to leave Salvador, he became a spokesperson for the Democratic Revolutionary Front in Washington and later California. We first met in the basement of a church in Washington in February 1981, when Mario spoke to about a dozen of us who had showed up for a public meeting to learn about the US-sponsored war in El Salvador. We worked together trying to stop U.S. interference in his country until May of 1992 and are friends to this day. Mario Velasquez is a man of vision and huge dreams of a better world for us all.

# LISA VENEKLASEN

*"How food and this recipe fit together...*

*Food is the ultimate peace and justice agenda in so many ways – it's about our relationship to nature, to communities and to each other. But I'm not going to write about why. Instead, this recipe embodies a different kind of rhythm and connection we search for as peace and justice activists.*

*As a long-time, extremely hectic peace and justice activist, sometimes I wonder how we resolve the inevitable conflicts that surround and inhabit us through peaceful means when our personal and public lives are such a mad race of impossible juggling and....well, conflict. For me even the task of cooking food in the evening for my family generates tension because I don't have time often.*

*I love this recipe because I buy the acorn squash from a local farm and sometimes, the peas too. Other times, I'm lazy and get a can (woops – not such a good relationship with nature). It's so easy to make that I can have a glass of wine and chat with my son while it's baking. It's so sweet and satisfying and simple to eat. It doesn't produce a lot of dirty dishes. Dirty dishes are definitely a source, albeit minor, of conflict. It reduces the problem of time as a source of conflict and that's just plain peaceful. Enjoy."*

## The Ultimate Comfort Squash

*Ingredients:*

**½ acorn squash per person**
**Petit pois (little peas – a can if you're in a hurry)**
**Brown sugar**
**Butter**

*Preparation:*

1. Preheat oven to 350°F.

2. Cut acorn squash in half and place on cookie sheet. Bake face down for 40-45 minutes.

3. In the meantime, cook the peas – if they're fresh, boil them in an inch of water until soft. If they're from a can, simply heat them up.

4. After the squash is ready, pull it out and turn each one over so that the little "bowl" is face up.

5. Put a big tab of butter and a teaspoon of brown sugar in the bowl. Let it melt together.

6. Put a scoop of peas on top in the little bowl. Serve and enjoy.

## About the Contributor...

Lisa Veneklasen is the founder and executive director of Just Associates (JASS), her latest endeavour to bring peace, justice and gender equality to the world. She's another brilliant organizer – you'll find a few others in this cookbook – who can make you laugh out loud with her killer sense of humor and make you want to scream just as loud with her sharp analysis of the injustices in the world. She and her band of colleagues have taken Just Associates from an idea to a vibrant international network of feminist activists, scholars, and popular educators in more than twenty-five countries. Grounded in local and national action, Just Associates works to strengthen the voice, visibility, and collective organizing power of women to create a just world.

We've known each other for a long time. Lisa hired me in 1984 just after I barely escaped from Johns Hopkins School of Advanced International Studies with master's degree in hand and we worked together trying to educate American citizens about US folly in Nicaragua. But that's another story, full of many other stories. To learn more about Lisa and her work with Just Associates, check out: www.justassociates.org.

# MARY WAREHAM

*"These little sweet cakes go nicely with the coffee we drink frequently to sustain our campaigning against cluster bombs. The recipe originates in France, but cafés across Aotearoa New Zealand have started to serve them. This recipe has been adapted for use in U.S. kitchens."*

## Friands
## (Sweet Cakes)

*Ingredients:*

1¾ cups confectioner's sugar ("icing" sugar in NZ)
⅓ cup plain white flour
½ teaspoon baking powder (optional, not essential)
1 cup almond meal (ground almonds in a food processor)
5 egg whites, room temperature
1 tablespoon unsalted butter, melted
A punnet (small basket) of berries (raspberry, strawberry, blueberry...)
Handful of dark chocolate baking chips

*Preparation:*

1. Preheat oven to 375°F.

2. Sift sugar, baking powder, and flour into a large mixing bowl then add almond meal; stir to combine.

3. Lightly beat egg whites and gradually stir into the mixture.

4. Melt butter in microwave and stir into the mixture.

5. Spoon approximately 2 tablespoons of the mixture into a tray of muffin tins (or a friand tray if you have one).

6. Sprinkle a few raspberries and chocolate on the top. Bake for 20 minutes or until golden and springy to touch. Test the friand with a toothpick to see if it is cooked through.

7. Allow to cool 10 minutes before removing from the tins. Serve with coffee.

*"Like banning landmines or cluster munitions, this dessert requires careful preparation, sustained attention, and attractive presentation to achieve optimal results. As a cross-border campaigner the recipe originates in my home country of Aotearoa New Zealand (don't listen to what Australians argue), but the list of ingredients has been adapted for use in US kitchens. Back home this dessert best follows a Sunday dinner of roast lamb and three vegetables."*

## Pavlova for Peace

*Ingredients:*

**6 egg whites, room temperature**
**2 cups superfine sugar (caster sugar in NZ)**
**1 teaspoon vanilla essence**
**1 teaspoon malt vinegar**
**2 teaspoons corn starch (corn flour in NZ)**
**About 1½ cups cream, whipped**
**4 kiwifruit, peeled and sliced for decoration**
**Mint sprigs to garnish**

*Preparation:*

1. Preheat oven to 230°F (110°C).

2. Beat egg whites in a large bowl (not plastic) until soft peaks form.

3. Over a 10 minute period, gradually add the sugar, one tablespoon at a time. The mixture should become glossy, thick and shiny with each addition. Beat in vanilla essence, vinegar and corn flour. Spoon mixture out into a plate sized mound on a tray lined with parchment paper.

4. Bake for approximately 1½ hours until dry and crisp and lifts easily off the baking paper. Cool on a wire rack.

5. To serve, spread whipped cream on top and garnish with sliced kiwifruit and mint.

*(Editors' Note: There is some contention as to the origins of the "Pavlova." When Mairead Maguire sent her recipe, she wrote that it was from Russia, via Ireland, as you'll see in her contribution. Mary Wareham, however, wrote: "No way! It was named after a Russian ballerina but created by a New Zealand chef." Mary offered this weblink as her evidence: http://en.wikipedia.org/wiki/Pavlova_(food). Futher, a third! person sent in a recipe for Pavlova – Sr. Denise Coughlan, a fabulous member of the International Campaign to Ban Landmines, who is from Australia but who has lived for more than two decades in Cambodia, working with the Jesuit Refugee Service. We thought three Pavlova recipes might be too many...)*

## About the Contributor...

Mary Wareham currently – and again – works for Steve Goose at Human Rights Watch, where she uses her prodigous talents in the work banning cluster bombs and landmines. We first met the inimitable Ms. Wareham when she was a student from New Zealand doing research on the Landmine Campaign. Her trajectory led her to become head of the New Zealand Campaign to Ban Landmines and then to work with Jody Williams and then Steve Goose after she'd moved to Washington, DC. There was something of a hiatus when she returned home to New Zealand and took up work with Oxfam New Zealand. But apparently Mary Wareham's heart is with banning weapons and she's back at it albeit still from beautiful New Zealand. In her spare time, she put together a highly-recognized documentary on landmines, *Disarm!* and subsequently managed the logistics of the book, B*anning Landmines: Disarmament, Citizen Diplomacy and Human Security*, which she edited with Williams and Goose. Check out Mary in an interview about cluster bombs at: www.youtube.com/watch?v+VVdC2TbrG1M. For information about her film, go to: www.disarmfilm.org. You can find the book at Amazon.com.

# CORA WEISS

*"Peace is not the absence of war, but the presence of so many good things – just like a good recipe! The idea is to make a big fish soup with enough interesting ingredients to stimulate a conversation which will accompany your discussion about how to make peace happen. Bon appetite!"*

## Peace Soup

*Ingredients:*

Olive oil
Garlic
Onion
Fennel
Red, orange and green bell peppers; chopped
Chicken stock
Clam juice
1 bay leaf
Red or white wine (whichever is handy; there should be enough to make a good broth. If you don't use it up the first time, it keeps well for left-overs.)
Tomatoes
Potatoes
Salsa
Corn
Halibut, scrod, cod, bass, or any other weak (white, light) fish. (If you like shell fish, add shrimp, deveined and peeled, or crab, lobster or clams. Any kind of clams will do, but get the sand out before adding them to the soup at the last minute. )
Oregano, cumin; your favorite spices
Red pepper flakes to taste
Lemon juice to taste
Kosher salt to taste

## Preparation:

1. Start with a heavy pot, olive oil, garlic, onion, fennel, and add heat.
2. Add red, orange and green peppers.
3. Add chicken stock, clam juice, bay leaf, and a little wine.
4. Cut up tomatoes, dice some potatoes, find some salsa, and cut the kernels from some corn; add it to the sauce and stir.
5. Add fish.
6. Add oregano, cumin, and your favorite spices.
7. Add red pepper flakes to taste (depending on your taste for piquante).
8. Add more stock or juice; squeeze in lemons (or even an orange!). Kosher salt also adds flavor.

*For the side, warm a baguette and put garlic butter between the slices. A crispy green salad and a bottle of your favorite brew tops it off.*

## About the Contributor...

Cora Weiss is legendary, so it is extremely difficult to know where to begin! She has dedicated her life's work to peace, justice, disarmament and human rights. She is currently the President of the Hague Appeal for Peace, which is a network of organizations and individuals dedicated to ending war and making peace a human right. She has served as President of the International Peace Bureau, which received the Nobel Peace Prize in 1910; was a co-founder of Women Strike for Peace, which was involved in efforts to end atmospheric nuclear testing; and was a leader in the anti-Vietnam War movement. I first met the rather intimidating – at least to me at the time -- Ms. Weiss when she was chair of the board of the Nicaragua-Honduras Education Project, where I worked with Lisa Veneklasen, and which Cora had taken the lead in creating. Cora's family foundation was the very first to give me a grant when I began work to create the International Campaign to Ban Landmines so many years ago. You definitely want Cora Weiss as your ally in work to create a world of peace with justice and equality. You can find information about Cora and the Hague Appeal for Peace at: www.haguepeace.org.

# REVEREND DR. GLORIA WHITE-HAMMOND

*"These days, I do 'for real' cooking like three times a year – Easter, Thanksgiving and Christmas. Our family will tell you that the holiday just isn't right if they can't look forward to this banana cake for dessert. So go bananas and enjoy!"*

## Banana Cake Cockaigne

*Ingredients:*

Have all ingredients about 70°F.
Cake:

**2 cups flour – sift before measuring**
**½ teaspoon double-acting baking powder**
**¾ teaspoon baking soda**
**½ teaspoon salt**
**½ cup butter**
**1½ cups sifted sugar**
**2 eggs**
**1 cup lightly mashed ripe bananas**
**1 teaspoon vanilla**
**¼ cup yogurt or buttermilk**

Icing:

**¾ package cream cheese**
**3 tablespoons butter**
**Confectioner's sugar (to suit your taste)**
**Vanilla extract (to suit your taste)**
**Evaporated milk (enough to make the icing spreadable)**

*Preparation:*

*Cake:*

1. Preheat oven to 350°F.

2. Sift before measuring the two cups flour, then resift with baking powder, baking soda and salt.

3. Cream the butter and gradually add the sugar, creaming until light.

4. Beat in the eggs, one at a time.

5. Combine the cup of lightly mashed ripe bananas, the vanilla and the yogurt or buttermilk.

6. Add the flour mixture to the butter mixture in three parts, alternating with the banana mixture. Stir the batter after each addition until smooth.

7. Bake in greased and floured pans about 30 minutes.

If served at once, this cake is good with confectioner's sugar sprinkled on top; or with whipped cream. But my favorite topping is a...

*White Icing:*

1. Cream the cream cheese with the butter.
2. Stir in confectioner's sugar and vanilla extract to suit your taste.
3. Then add evaporated milk— enough to make the icing spreadable. Too much will make it runny--I know...I've been there and done that!
4. After spreading the icing on each layer, I slice ripe bananas and place them on top. To keep the bananas from turning brown, I squeeze a drop of lemon juice over each slice.

## About the Contributor...

The Reverend Dr. Gloria White-Hammond is a pastor and retired pediatrician who "lives, eats, and sleeps pondering ways to solve the genocide" in Darfur. After a trip to southern Sudan in 2001, where she took part in a mission to liberate 6,700 slaves, she returned to the US and helped found "My Sister's Keeper," whose mission is "focused on assisting, protecting and advocating for the women of southern Sudan who live in Gogrial County." Gloria is also on the Board of Directors of "Save Darfur," a coalition of non-governmental organization that works to end the war in Darfur. A gracious and generous woman, Gloria brought her world of experience on the situation in Sudan and Darfur to the Nobel Women's Initiative delegation to the region, as well as to the Thai/Burma border, in July-August 2008. For more information on the Rev. Dr. Gloria White-Hammond, please go to: www.mskeeper. org. You can also check out www.savedarfur.org. You can watch Gloria in action on videos at youtube.com.

# BETTY
# WILLIAMS

## Salmon in Pastry

*Ingredients:*

      2¾ pounds salmon, skinned and boned; cut into two filets
      ½ cup butter
      2 inches ginger, peeled and finely chopped
      1 tablespoon raisins (optional)
      8 ounces short-crust pastry (frozen if you can't make your own)
      1 egg yolk, beaten, to glaze

*Preparation:*

    1. Preheat oven to 425°F.

    2. Mix butter with ginger and raisins; spread on top of one piece of salmon.

    3. Put the other piece of salmon on top and press down gently.

    4. Season the salmon with salt and black pepper to taste.

    5. Roll out the pastry into a large piece.

    6. Put the salmon in the middle and wrap the pastry over the salmon, pressing the pastry closed into a package; trim off any bits of extra pastry, and pierce pastry in a few places to let steam escape.

    7. Brush with the beaten egg and bake for 30-35 minutes.

    8. Serve with hollandaise sauce.

*(Editors' Note: Find recipe for hollandaise sauce on page 37.)*

## About the Contributor...

Betty Williams received the Nobel Peace Prize in 1976 for her work as a co-founder of Community of Peace People, an organization dedicated to promoting a peaceful resolution to the troubles in Northern Ireland; co-founder Mairead Maguire also received the Peace Prize that year. Betty has a great deep laugh and devilish Irish sense of humor. She's formidable in her commitment to protecting and promoting the rights of children. She is founder and president of the World Centers of Compassion for Children International, whose mission is "to create a strong political voice for children in areas of stress due to war, hunger or social, economic, or political upheaval and to respond to their expressed nedds materially and emotionally." She is also one of the founders of the Nobel Women's Initiative along with sister Nobel Peace Laureates, who decided to bring together their experiences in a united effort to support women around the world working for peace with justice and equality. You'll find Betty Williams and more information about the World Centers of Compassion for Children International at: www.centersofcompassion.org.

# JODY WILLIAMS

*"Peace is not just the absence of war. It's a world with justice and equality. It's a world where the basic needs of the majority of the people on our planet are met. If we stop spending money on war and the weapons of war, we'd have more than enough to invest in these basics of long-term peace. People should have basic housing, access to medical care, education, and work. Everyone should have clean drinking water and food to eat every day.*

*One of the joys of life is sharing food with those we love. Everyone should have enough to be able to do that. In our family, we love to cook and experiment with cooking and enjoy each other over a good meal. I hope you like these recipes."*

## South Asian Meatloaf

*Ingredients:*

Meatloaf:

- ¾ cup minced onion
- ½ cup minced celery
- ½ cup minced carrot
- ¼ cup minced green pepper
- ¼ cup minced red pepper
- 3 large cloves minced garlic
- 1 teaspoon salt (optional)
- ¼ teaspoon black pepper
- ½ teaspoon white pepper
- ¼ teaspoon ground nutmeg
- 1½ tablespoons garam masala
- ½ cup fat-free half and half
- ½ cup ketchup
- 1 pound lean ground beef
- 1 pound ground lamb
- 1 beaten egg
- ¾ cup dry bread crumbs

*Au juice:*

> **4 minced shallots**
> **2 tablespoons butter**
> **1 sprig thyme**
> **1 bay leaf**
> **Dash of crushed or coarse ground black pepper**
> **1 cup dry white wine**
> **1 cup beef stock**
> **1 cup chicken stock**
> **1½ teaspoons garam masala**

## Preparation:

*Meatloaf:*

1. Preheat oven to 350°F.

2. Sauté onion, celery, carrot, green pepper, red pepper, and garlic. Then set aside to cool. (If you're feeling a bit lazy, you can microwave them until hot and then set aside to cool.)

3. Mix together salt, cayenne, black pepper, white pepper, cumin, nutmeg, and garam masala.

4. Add half and half, ketchup, ground beef, lamb, egg, the sautéed and cooled vegetables, and bread crumbs to the spices.

5. Make sure all the ingredients are well combined.

6. Form into a loaf and place in a greased baking pan.

7. Cover with tin foil and bake for about 30 minutes; remove foil and continue baking for 15-20 minutes.

8. Remove from oven and let stand for 10 minutes before slicing. Serve au juice.

*Au Juice:*

1. Sauté shallots in 1 tablespoon butter with thyme, bay leaf, black pepper and garam masala.

2. Add white wine and simmer over high heat until reduced to glaze.

3. Add beef and chicken stocks and simmer over high heat until reduced by ⅓ or ½.

4. Stir in remaining butter and season to taste with salt and pepper. Discard bay leaf.

*We tend to serve this with mashed potatoes, with the sauce on the potatoes as well as the meat. Rice or baked potatoes would be good too. A nice, spicy wine such as a gewürztraminer goes very nicely with this dish.*

# Fantastic Bourbon Apple Pie

*Ingredients:*

**9-inch pie crust**
**7 Granny Smith apples**
**3 tablespoons bourbon (preferably Marker's Mark)**
**1½ cups sugar**
**1 tablespoon cinnamon**
**½ cup flour**
**½ cup crushed walnuts**
**½ cup butter**

*Preparation:*

1. Preheat oven to 425°F.

2. Lightly brown the crust; set aside to cool.

3. Peel, core and slice 7 Granny Smith apples into a saucepan.

4. Add bourbon, 1 cup of the sugar and cinnamon. Cook until slightly tender. Pour into the pie shell.

5. Combine ½ cup sugar, flour, walnuts and butter. Mix until crumbly.

6. Cover apples with topping.

7. Cook 25-30 minutes.

*Serve warm with cheddar cheese, vanilla ice cream or whipped cream.*

## About the Contributor...

Jody Williams was awarded the 1997 Nobel Peace Prize jointly with the International Campaign to Ban Landmines for her effort to ban landmines and currently serves as a Campaign Ambassador. She speaks powerfully to people of all ages and travels worldwide advocating for a peaceful and violence-free world. Jody co-founded the Nobel Women's Initiative with sister Nobel Peace Laureates Shirin Ebadi, Wangari Maathai, Rigoberta Menchú Tum, Betty Williams, and Mairead Maguire in January 2006. The Nobel Women's Initiative promotes the effort of women's rights activists to advance peace with justice and equality for women and all peoples in this world. Jody works with a goal of empowering women - pushing them to realize that they are all capable of changing our world. She is also active with PeaceJam, an organization that unites youth with Peace Laureates. In 2007, she was the head of a controversial High-Level Mission dispatched by the Human Rights Council to report on the situation of human rights in Darfur and the needs of Sudan. Jody Williams is also professor at the Graduate College of Social Work at the University of Houston. For more information, check out: www.nobelwomensinitiative.org.

# ZEINA ZAATARI

*"An age-old recipe from the coastal city of Sign, Lebanon, where we are told the locals have over 100 recipes for cooking eggplant. This dish can be eaten as a vegetarian main meal, as a side dish, or as an appetizer at parties (more commonly known in the USA as a dip). When cooking, always follow your heart rather than a recipe! Enjoy!"*

## The Perfect Baba Ghanouj

*Ingredients:*

**1 large eggplant**
**1 clove of garlic**
**A dash of salt**
**½ lemon**
**2 tablespoons yogurt**
**2 tablespoons Tahini (a sesame seed syrup/paste that can be found in international food stores or food co-ops in the US)**

*Preparation:*

*To prepare:*

1. Bake and peel eggplant.
2. Mash garlic and add to eggplant.
3. Mix in salt, lemon, yogurt and Tahini, mashing throughout the process.
4. Place on a plate; decorate.

*To serve:*

5. Chop parsley for decoration.
6. Top with a little olive oil to taste.
7. Serve with pita bread.

*Helpful Tips to Remember:*
- Remember to poke eggplant before baking to avoid explosion.
- Make sure to remove all eggplant juice before adding other ingredients, so you do not have a soggy Baba Ghanouj.
- Use a garlic wooden crusher/mortar to mash eggplant and mix ingredients for better texture. Warm the pita bread slightly before serving.
- You can use sour red pomegranates or radishes for decoration instead of or in addition to parsley for decoration. All taste and look good with Baba Ghanouj.
- Salt, yogurt, Tahini, garlic, and lemon are up to individual taste.

## About the Contributor...

Dr. Zeina Zaatari is a program officer for the Middle East and North Africa at the Global Fund for Women, which supports women's groups around the world in their work for equality and social justice. She is a cultural anthropologist who received her Ph.D. from the University of California at Davis. Zeina teaches, lectures and writes about Arab and Muslim women, women and war, and Arab American feminism, among many other subjects. She also produces a radio program on the Middle East and North Africa. Not one to waste time, Zeina also is a founding member of the Radical Arab Women's Activist Network, the National Council of Arab Americans, and Sunbula: Arab Feminists for Change in the Bay Area, California. For more information, check out: www.globalfundforwomen.org.

# QING ZHANG

## Shrimp Balls in Tofu
### *(Serves two)*

*Ingredients:*

**½ pound uncooked shrimp**
**14-ounce package firm tofu**
**1 egg**
**⅛ teaspoon salt (or to taste)**
**14½ ounces of chicken or vegetable broth**

*Preparation:*

1. Peel the shrimp and chop into fine pieces (or use food processor).

2. In a mixing bowl, combine the shrimp, egg and salt.

3. Cut tofu into 2-inch squares, about 1-inch deep. Using a tablespoon, scoop out tofu in the center of each piece to create little bowl-like indentations in the tofu where the shrimp mixture will go. If you want, you can add the excess tofu to the shrimp mixture.

4. Scoop a tablespoon of the shrimp mixture to form a small ball and place it in the indentations in each piece of tofu.

5. Pour chicken broth into a shallow pan on top of the stove; broth should be approximately ½ inch deep. Place filled tofu squares in the broth. Bring to boil, then cover the pan and reduce heat; simmer for 10 minutes.

*Serve and enjoy!*

## About the Contributor...

Qing Zhang is a an activist in China who works with migrant workers, many of whom are women. She is dedicated to working to see that their human rights are observed. Qing was a member of the Nobel Women's Initiative delegation to the Thai/Burma border, Ethiopia, South Sudan and Chad in July-August 2008. Her easy manner, warmth and broad smile added calm and balance to the group. Her insights into the challenges facing migrant workers was very valuable, particularly in Thailand, where most of the refugees from Burma are undocumented migrants. For more information about the delegation, please go to: www.nobelwomensinitiative.org.

pea